The Kissinger Saga

The Kissinger Saga

Walter and Henry Kissinger
Two brothers from Fürth

EVI KURZ

Weidenfeld & Nicolson
LONDON

First published in Great Britain in 2009
by Weidenfeld & Nicolson

Originally published in German in 2007 by
TLF TimeLineFilm GmbH, Fürth, under the title
Die Kissinger Saga

1 3 5 7 9 10 8 6 4 2

A CIP catalogue record for this book
is available from the British Library.

ISBN-13 978 0 297 85875 7

Typeset by Input Data Services Ltd, Bridgwater, Somerset

**Printed in the UK by
CPI William Clowes Beccles NR34 7TL**

The Orion Publishing Group's policy is to use papers that
are natural, renewable and recyclable products and made
from wood grown in sustainable forests. The logging and
manufacturing processes are expected to conform to
the environmental regulations of the country of origin.

Grateful acknowledgement is made to Northwestern
University Press for permission to reproduce Heinrich
Heine's poem 'Wither Now?' from *Songs of Love and
Grief* (1995), translated by Walter W. Arndt

Weidenfeld & Nicolson

The Orion Publishing Group Ltd
Orion House
5 Upper Saint Martin's Lane
London, WC2H 9EA

An Hachette UK company

www.orionbooks.co.uk

To my daughters Anja and Katharina

Contents

Preface

This book contains two stories. They belong together. The first deals with the lives lived by two brothers who grew up in Germany between the world wars, who were forced to leave their home during the Nazi era, who forged great careers for themselves in America, and yet still return time and again to their home in Franconia.

The second story deals with the stages of my unusual route to finding the two men. Never before have Henry and Walter Kissinger talked about their private life. By doing so now, by telling their life story to me, the journalist from their Franconian home town of Fürth, they opened up a new chapter in my own life.

Many people, in many different ways, helped this book to come into being – librarians and archivists, relations, friends, colleagues and travelling companions of the two brothers, but the brothers themselves more than anyone. Without the conversations that I was able to have with them, and without the documents that they put at my disposal, their story could never have been written. And my own story would be that much the poorer. So my very special, personal thanks go out to Henry and Walter Kissinger.

Evi Kurz
Fürth, March 2007

How I looked for Henry and Walter

Then I do it I write the letter. I've been hesitating for a long time – days, weeks, months. It's been a time of doubt – in me, my subject, the brothers. Because I've never met them. One of them, of course, I know from a distance, from television. For as long as I can remember, Henry Kissinger has been on the screen, as statesman, Nobel laureate, adviser. Once I was quite close to him in reality, in May 1998, when he was made an honorary citizen of the city of Fürth.

Sometimes it seems to me as if that event happened only yesterday, the memory is so vivid. I was deeply moved, by his speech and by the letter that Henry Kissinger read out on that occasion. It had been written by his mother, when she was almost a hundred years old. Its lines spoke of her deep connection with the city, where she had married and given birth to her two sons, even though she and her family had been expelled from Fürth by the Nazis.

Since then, I haven't been able to get that scene out of my mind. And over time it has turned into the idea of getting to the bottom of that story. I want to capture it, record it in a television documentary while it is still possible to do so. While Henry Kissinger is still able to tell the story. He is now approaching eighty, and sprightly and quick-witted though he still is, the time will come when he is no longer able to talk about what happened back then.

But he isn't just any old eye-witness. Internationally, Henry Kissinger is one of the most in-demand and best-paid figures in public life. And until now he has strictly refused to talk to the camera about his private life. What have I got to offer? Of course, Henry Kissinger has never heard of me before. But mightn't that be an advantage? A stroke of luck? And besides, we have one thing in common: the place we come from. We both grew up in Fürth.

The months pass and the whole business gradually fades from my mind. But not from my heart. And then chance comes to my aid. Early in 2003, when I am researching a local story, I discover that Henry has a brother: Walter Kissinger, a good year younger than Henry. Strange that he is completely unknown, at least hereabouts. Whoever I speak to over the next few months, almost everyone, even Helmut Schmidt, an old friend of Henry Kissinger's, says, 'What? Henry has a brother?'

And Walter Kissinger has a great career behind him in America; among other things he spent almost twenty years at the head of the Allen Group, a major technological concern. So he is a heavyweight as well. Will I get to talk to him? He doesn't have such a complex and complicated relationship with the media as his brother Henry does. Perhaps he would be willing to let me have a few memories from his old home town in Germany. And his brother Henry will be turning eighty at the end of May. A film about the family history would be a lovely gift.

So I write the letter. I am sure of my subject, or at least of the idea of it. Everything else stops me sleeping at night. The people I tell about my idea all think it is a mistake. My family thinks I have gone completely crazy; however, my two daughters are past the difficult stage, they are more or less grown-up, so my hands are free.

At first, what I have in mind is a six- to seven-minute film for Bayerisches Fernsehen, for the *Frankenschau* programme. But my boss says no; he says he is sure that 'no one's interested in Kissinger'. If he has a different view of things three years later, that's his problem. The head of television in Munich isn't interested either. Bayerischer Rundfunk made a film about Henry

Kissinger only five years ago. OK, I think, then I'll do it on my own. For the first time in my life, I won't just be filming a ninety-minute documentary on my own, I'll produce the film myself. In short, I'll be looking to new professional horizons.

Above all, I've decided to put the Kissinger brothers on camera. I want to get them talking. I want the two of them to look back on their lives. Will they play along? It's quite amazing that no one's ever had the idea of telling the story. I know, of course, that it's too late for the occasion itself: Henry turns eighty in six weeks. But it's now or never. That birthday could be the opportunity to make the film.

On 15 April 2003 I write a long letter to Walter Kissinger, introducing myself and my project. I write in German. I don't feel confident enough in English to get the tone right, and I am also working on the basis that Walter is bound not to have forgotten his mother tongue, or will at least still understand it.

'My name is Evi Kurz, I've lived in Fürth since I was born there in 1955, I trained as a teacher, and for twenty-four years I've worked as a television journalist for Bayerisches Fernsehen, in particular for the magazine series *Franconiaschau*, which deals with the region and its people ... Our *Franconiaschau* programme reaches a million viewers a week and, with a market share of 24 per cent, we are one of the highest-rating programmes on Bavarian television ... I would like to take your brother's eightieth birthday as an opportunity to make a personal portrait of your family, which has had its roots in Franconia for centuries ... May I dare to hope that you will accompany me on part of my quest?'

Will Walter reply? He does, in English. Just two lines, an email. But it's a reaction. He wants to think about my letter, and he will let me know. And then, early in May, a letter arrives from America. In it I find photocopied pages from *Who's Who in America*, giving details about the Kissinger brothers, a slightly more complete CV for Walter, some childhood photographs of

Henry and Walter, the text of a speech that his father gave in Fürth in 1975, and a letter. It's a reply to my request.

In it Walter mentions the village of Leutershausen, his mother's birthplace, and he speaks of her closest friends, Karl and Babby Hezner. They alone had kept alive the connection with a time when everyone else had severed their friendships with the Kissingers' mother: 'It's a miracle that Karl Hezner survived the Nazi period.' Even now, he, Walter Kissinger, and his brother Henry are in close contact with the Hezners' two daughters, their childhood playmates. He also gives me their addresses, and suggests the possibility of a personal conversation should I come to New York.

Is this the breakthrough? Will I get the chance to talk to Walter, and also with his brother Henry? If I'd had any idea what a long journey I had ahead of me, that in Walter's case it wouldn't be until August 2004, and in Henry's case April 2005, that they would be willing to talk in front of a camera about themselves and their lives, I'd have given up long ago. But I stick at it, because I am still in correspondence with Walter, because I've made contact with Henry, and because over the next few months I will be able to meet both of them.

In retrospect, I wonder where I found the strength and the patience. Even Walter's attempt to talk to Henry about the project, and then to put me in the picture, became an endurance test, because the famous brother was constantly on the move. Where did he get the energy? At any rate we had that in common – that and our home in Franconia.

Eventually I get Walter ready with emails and news from Fürth and the surrounding area. He then suggests a meeting in London and, by way of preparation, a phone call, and I am as excited as a child at Christmas. Our first telephone conversation happens on 26 May, in which he surprises me with his calm and pleasant manner and, as far as I can judge, his elegant, unaccented English. Quite unlike his brother Henry, who never shook off his underlying Franconian melody, perhaps because he never wanted to.

In passing, Walter mentions that his brother will be spending his eightieth birthday 'very close by'. It's as if I am electrified: does that mean Henry has grown sentimental about the old days, that this important birthday is drawing him back to his homeland in Franconia? And if that's the case, where will he go? To his beloved grandfather's grave? It's worth a try. I know that Henry would go there every time he visited the city. Perhaps that would be a chance for an interview? So I keep a cameraman ready, just in case, set off for Fürth's Jewish cemetery, the 'new' one on Erlanger Strasse, and wait for Henry Kissinger and my opportunity. Eight hours, in vain. Henry was indeed 'very close by' – but close to his brother Walter, in New York.

I am down, but not out. On the contrary. It was a big, intense experience inspired by the very best intentions, and I get home to an email from Walter. In it he confirms our meeting in London: Monday, 2 June, 11.30 a.m., in the Harrington Hall Hotel, South Kensington. I travel the evening before and book myself in just round the corner.

Fifteen minutes before the agreed time I am waiting in the Harrington Hall, watching an elderly lady walking twice across the lobby and back to the lift. No sign of Walter. I start getting nervous. After I ask for Mr Kissinger at reception, the same lady appears for a third time and is surprised to learn that I am Evi Kurz, the one with whom the meeting has been arranged. They'd been expecting someone older.

Eugenie Kissinger, known as Genie – I've met her now, and liked her immediately – leads me up to the fourth floor. It's one of those typical English hotels, with long, narrow corridors, twisting and turning round lots of corners, decorated with those familiar shaggy, brightly coloured, tasteless carpets. Walter isn't at the door to welcome us. He is waiting in a wing chair that forms part of a suite at the very back of the room.

First impressions are surprising, not to say disappointing. I'd imagined Walter differently, as a wiry, elegantly dressed, tall, senior-management type. But the man sitting there in his chair, wearing casual trousers and a checked shirt, looks small, almost weedy. His narrow face is dominated by an unusually large pair of glasses. His posture looks strained, not least because Walter is crouching in his chair, as if lying in wait for something. Throughout our conversation he grips tightly the arms of his chair.

Today I know that that first impression was wrong, that Walter was nervous and tense, and that he was tense because of the subject of our conversation. The better I got to know him, the more open, warm and easy I found him to be. About five foot eight inches tall, the eighty-year-old isn't a small man. He holds himself upright, looks almost athletic, his speech is plain and his words well chosen, and he unobtrusively reveals himself to be a very intelligent person. Walter is confident and at the same time remarkably lacking in vanity. He knows about his successes, and he also knows how they came about. And his brother Henry had nothing to do with it. He is self-contained and authentic, and that in itself creates an effect.

The fine facial features, the alert eyes, the winning, always reticent smile, do the rest. Walter has charm. I soon sense that he is prudent, considerate and attentive. Genie confirms as much – later, in front of the camera – and tells me that for that reason her whole life has been a very happy one. And you also sense that Walter knows what a wonderful wife he has, when you see the two of them together. She always makes sure he has plenty of space; and Genie is there the first time Walter talks to me about himself and his brother.

The atmosphere is tense. Walter knows that he has taken the first step along a particular path, and that he doesn't know where it will lead. Just as he doesn't know exactly who this person is, sitting opposite him in a London hotel room. Why did I write to him and not his brother, the one I am actually interested in? 'Because I don't think Henry ever read my letter, I think he threw it straight in the waste-paper basket.' Did that mean I wanted to get to Henry through him?

I do my best to convince Walter of my true intentions, and to make it plain that I want to paint a portrait of the whole family, not just of Henry, that I also want to give an account of him, Walter, and not least of their parents, Louis and Paula Kissinger. Of course, a conversation with Henry would be part of that as well. At last, he says I should write a letter to Henry and send it to him. He will meet his brother and make sure he reads my letter. Then we go out for lunch.

Things remain strained – he is nervous, and so am I. He brought me a few newspaper cuttings about himself and his career. I give him a book of pictures of old Fürth and a little book containing the childhood memories of Robert Schopflocher. He is the same age as the Kissinger brothers, he too grew up in Fürth, and he and his family were also driven from the city. The three of them never really met, but Walter is visibly delighted by this message from long ago.

Then, when I give him copies from the police files documenting his family's expulsion from Fürth, Walter turns as white as chalk, begins to shake and prepares to say goodbye: he is sorry that he hasn't more time to spare, but he has a very full schedule. The goodbye itself is very warm, and in spite of all the tension and his rather abrupt departure, I am sure we'll be seeing each other again. I've got a good feeling about it.

But I am irritated, of course, and I don't like my hotel. After I've swapped it for one where I feel more at ease, and after I've left Walter a message to that effect, I go out, first to the Holocaust exhibition at the Imperial War Museum, then to the home of an Orthodox Jew whose family also came from Fürth, and last of all to the theatre. But I can't concentrate. My thoughts are still with Walter.

Because my mobile phone is switched off, I don't get his request to call him back until late that evening: he wants me to join him and his Harvard friends on an outing to Churchill's home at Chartwell, and I'll need my passport to get through security. When we speak the next morning, as he says goodbye he adds, 'From now on, you don't just have a place in my mind, you're in my heart as well.'

So I take the next step. I write to Henry, a lot of closely written pages – about me, my work, my plans: 'I want it to be a sympathetic, warm-hearted portrait that starts in Franconia, where your family has had its roots for centuries ... I am not one of those famous, award-winning journalists from all over the world ... People in Franconia know me. For them, for twenty-four years I've been a face that they like to look at, a face they trust ... I am not a political journalist. I don't want to uncover any so-called scandals, I don't want to convict anybody ... Let me, as a lifelong resident of Fürth, tell the story of your family. Give me, as your brother did, the chance for us to get to know each other.'

My letter is despatched on 13 July, to Walter, who, as promised, puts it into Henry's hand. Then the long wait begins all over again. I use the time to develop my story, I conduct interviews at home, I work in archives and visit the villages where the family has its roots, and where their ancestors are buried. But, of course, I keep my eye on America as well: in a dozen emails and letters to Walter I try to find out whether and when I might expect his brother to agree to an interview. He probes as best he can, but by late July he is 'no longer optimistic', and in mid-August he is trying to keep me happy with pictures of his wife, his sons, daughters-in-law and grandchildren.

Then, in late August 2003, Henry's reply suddenly arrives. It's a yes, although only to a short interview in October. With

9

the best will in the world, there's no more than that – he has engagements, as I must know: in Russia, China, and who knows where else in the world. Besides, he '*never* gives interviews' about his 'private life'. But he is touched by the fact that I've devoted so much energy and devotion to the project. He is also astonished at the amount of material I've managed to collect. Could I give any insights to a German historian he wanted to employ to research his family tree?

In retrospect, I am surprised at my naivety. As if the film was in the bag just because he'd said yes! Certainly, there's a date for a double interview with the brothers: at the end of the first weekend in October, in Henry Kissinger's New York office. What's missing is a film team and a production company. I have to make my mind up, and I have to act, quickly and consistently. Where the team is concerned, it's important to find the right people for the job and to get hold of work visas for the USA.

Considerably more time-consuming is the decision to set up my own company, TLF-TimeLineFilm GmbH. I'd made that step dependent on Henry's agreement to participate, and I've got that now. It doesn't help that we are about to go on a family holiday to Sardinia which I booked ages ago. The atmosphere is as you might imagine: I stake a claim to one of the rooms and use it as an office, I only ever show my face at mealtimes. By the end of the holiday I am absolutely exhausted, but it's done: the company has been set up, the German film crew is booked, the visas are on the way, flights and hotels are booked.

I've even found a lovely present for the two men – two Fürth caskets, specially made from the wood of a 150-year-old Fürth beech tree. The engraved dedications are dated October 2003, the time scheduled for the planned double interview with Henry and Walter Kissinger. They are both visibly touched, and say so, when I hand over their little presents – to Walter in June 2004, to Henry in April 2005.

That's because our appointment in October 2003 comes to

nothing. At the end of September, Henry tells me he has to move the date because of an unforeseen change in his plans, and could I please get in touch with his office to make a new one. I am not alone in being irritated, Walter is too. Plainly, the two brothers are at loggerheads. At least, that's what I hear from a telephone conversation with a very cross Walter Kissinger. It looks very much as if his brother has backed out – because he doesn't trust me, because he has been bitten by journalists before, and because he has come to suspect that his highly cooperative brother might play a bigger part in my film than Henry himself.

I am completely worn out. But I am also determined not to leave things there. I've never given up. So I start filming, in Germany. I've scheduled interviews with former pupils of Louis Kissinger, Henry and Walter's father, and also with the long-standing German ambassador to Washington, Berndt von Staden, who knows Henry very well and is also acquainted with Walter. I keep the brothers up to date about all that. So the weeks and months pass, with the occasional misunderstandings that inevitably arise out of transatlantic conversations and correspondence.

With the winter break, the dialogue freezes up. Walter's in California and can only be contacted again from the middle of March 2004. The new round begins as the old one stopped, with emails, letters, phone calls, and with a fresh misunderstanding: at the beginning of May, when the mayor of Fürth talks to me about Henry Kissinger's visit to the city, planned for 7 June – which I knew about, didn't I? – I am dumbstruck. I ask Walter about it. He says he doesn't know anything. Henry had mentioned that he was going to Germany at the beginning of June, and travelling on from there to China, but that was the usual routine.

Don't let it show, but it's getting difficult. The next blow

11

comes two weeks later, once again from the busy mayor, who has, of course, no idea what effect his news will have: Henry isn't coming to Fürth on his own, but with his brother Walter. This time I really can't believe it, and I know one thing: either I win on 7 June, or I've lost everything.

The weeks until then are an emotional roller coaster. First, Walter calls to tell me that he and Henry are coming to Germany. He is surprised that I know. He says it's a 'sentimental journey', a trip by the brothers to explore the traces of their childhood on the occasion of Henry's eightieth birthday. I like the idea.

Then Mayor Thomas Jung bestirs himself again and tells me that Dr Kissinger's office has been in touch with him again: 'Evi Kurz' should only attend the press conference that's been organized, and not, as originally planned, lunch in the Kartoffel restaurant. I am bitterly disappointed, feel I've been snubbed, and wonder whether that was his intention – whether Henry K. wants to hurt me. I also say that to Walter on the phone, before going to bed at five in the afternoon and pulling the covers over my head. The next day the emotional journey continues, and once again the mayor is, unwittingly, in the driving seat of the ghost train: the Kissinger office expressly asks the city of Fürth to invite me, and me alone, to dinner with the brothers.

And along comes 7 June. I go first to the hairdresser, then to my wardrobe, choose the bright-pink box dress and set off for the Kartoffel. They are already sitting round the table – in the middle, with their backs to the door: Henry and Walter, framed by bodyguards. The mayor – who else? – comes up to me, leads me over to Henry, and introduces me. He gives me a friendly hello, and studies me keenly. Walter beams from ear to ear. It's all very cordial, but we are still reticent: Henry sees and hears everything. Of course I know that without Walter's massive intervention I would never have met his brother. Clearly he didn't want Henry to snub me – and him – again.

*

So I meet Henry for the first time. I know him, of course. Everyone knows Henry. Henry's a star. At least since his meteoric rise to become Richard Nixon's security adviser in the late sixties, he has been a constant presence all over the world, and on German television screens as well. Fame and power have their price. In that respect Henry Kissinger is no different from any other VIP. He is under permanent observation, above all in America. For almost four decades, legions of journalists have lain in wait for him, waiting for ill-considered comments at unobserved moments, hoped for signs of weakness, searched for clues to his personality – always in search of the 'real' Henry.

I know all of that when I meet him for the first time. In that respect, my image of Henry is much more precise than the one I had of Walter before I met him. And here, too, I find I am surprised. Above all, he is more of a physical presence than I had imagined. About five foot eight inches tall, like his brother, Henry is clearly stouter, more massive than Walter. His slightly hunched shoulders give him a rather bullish appearance. His full face, with its snow-white hair and high forehead, is, as ever, dominated by the horn-rimmed glasses without which Henry Kissinger would be unimaginable. And today, as always, he is wearing them slightly crooked. Clearly that is one of his trademarks. Seeing them resting at a slight angle on his nose, it would be easy to underestimate him. And perhaps that's exactly what he wants.

Seeing him standing there, you wouldn't take him for an American. If I didn't know any better, I'd say a German Jew. And at least the way he talks, and also the cadence of his voice, reveal his German, *Fränkisch* origins. Henry's English is precise, nuanced and deliberate; even today he speaks with a slight accent. What is interesting is that the English accent in Henry's German is wearing off the older he becomes. Along with his

13

sonorous voice, language is another of his unmistakable trade-marks. You know who's talking, even if you don't see the man.

Of course, anyone who's been in the business for so long, anyone who has stood in the spotlight as long as this man, knows and controls the part he plays. So I assume quite naturally that the side of him that I meet first is the staged one. But I very soon see that Henry is actually just as he seems – charming, winning and incidentally, very humorous. From that point of view he is, like his brother, authentic. That goes for the public Henry at least, the professional.

But of course you don't see everything, because Henry doesn't show everything. The people he allows near him sense what he doesn't show. In this way I get to know a man who can be very emotional and very sentimental, not least where his origins, his family and his German homeland are concerned. Then one discovers how soft and sensitive he is, and one becomes aware of the energies he has mobilized to cover it up, as a matter of routine, all through his life. No wonder the shutters come down so often when Henry's origins are discussed: to talk about them would be to reveal his cover, and for such a man that would be a risky business.

On that memorable day, 7 June 2004, when I first meet him, I start to understand that. In the Kartoffel in Fürth I am seated opposite Henry, and after we have sat over asparagus, bratwurst and fried potatoes, talking about this and that, and about Fürth and its history, Henry first pays me a compliment: he thinks I know more about his family than he does himself. Then says he is sorry about the difficulties I encountered when trying to arrange a time to talk to him, but he is going to give me an interview. Not here and now, but later, in America. But he is going to let me have it. Full stop.

Then, when we talk about his father and family, his neighbours and friends, Henry asks me if I have any pictures. 'Yes.' Have I got them with me? 'Yes.' Can he look at them? 'Yes.' Now? 'Yes.' I rummage in my bag, which I packed that morning with this in mind, and show him some things from my collection, not just pictures, of which I don't yet have very many. It's amazing that Henry mixes up some of his father's pupils with relatives, and stoutly insists that this one is one aunt, that one another.

When the time has come for the press conference, he says I can ask my questions now. 'No.' When he insists, and I stick to my guns, he looks at me in bafflement, but doesn't say anything. Walter, to whom I can speak briefly on his own, is happy and contented: the miracle has happened, he says, and I am the one who brought it about.

After the press conference there's a tour of the city, with a big entourage. I stay in the background. Not until they are about to leave do I go to the car to say goodbye. Henry, who sees me coming over, gets out, smiles at me and says, 'I am glad we have met. You will have the interview. Not here in Fürth, but in New York, perhaps in Berlin. But you'll have it.' I am happy. I like Henry.

And I am getting closer and closer to Walter. The next day we meet in Bamberg, four days later in Leutershausen, at the home of Erika Bickert, the daughter of the Hezners, who were the only ones to stay in touch with the Kissingers after 1933. For the first and only time I hear Walter speaking a bit of German. Then, when he mentions Henry, he calls him 'Heinz'. That was his brother's name before they left Germany. I am very moved by that.

Have I reached my goal? Or am I about to get there? Admittedly, there's no news from Henry, or at least I haven't been given a date. I have, on the other hand, had an invitation from Walter and his wife Genie to their ranch in Colorado. That's where the

The promise: Fürth, 7 June 2004.

first interview with the younger of the two brothers is to take place. I set off on 26 August 2004, with a camera crew, full of hope, but also with the anxious question of whether the interview will be a good one. At the same time it becomes clear to me that Henry's refusal has its good side: both men together in front of the camera, in Henry's office, and in two thirty-minute takes – it wouldn't have worked. So, to Walter.

At about three o'clock we are in Denver, from there by hire car to Colorado Springs. I am staying at the Broadmoor, a recommendation of Walter's. Next morning Genie comes to collect me. The ranch is at an altitude of 9,000 feet. They spent three years looking for this place. When they first came to Colorado they fell in love with the landscape. In 1994 they found what they were looking for. The Lazy K Ranch abuts a national park, and that gives Walter the chance to ride as far as sixty miles to the west or north without encountering any traces of modern civilization.

Because rain is bucketing down and mist is rolling up as I get there, at first there isn't much to be seen. Walter is waiting at the top of the hill, dressed like a cowboy. His greeting is warm and personal; on the way there Genie had warned me that they were expecting guests, and because no one here understands the form of address normally used in Germany, 'Herr So-and-So', 'Frau So-and-So', we are immediately on first-name terms. Now I am no longer Frau Kurz. I am Evi now.

When the guests arrive for the aforementioned party – an agreeable, informal gathering in the late afternoon – the interview is already behind us. I am allowed to stay at the ranch, in a big apartment in the basement, which has a shelf full of photograph albums. Walter has told me I can look through them. Since I'd like to do that with him, but the opportunity never presents itself, nothing comes of it: I resist the temptation of doing it alone. Later I regret my shyness.

Naturally, I get to know them quite well during our time

together, including Genie, who is of Dutch extraction. I've rarely met a woman who can be as winning from the very first moment as Walter's wife. The natural, sincere way in which she approaches me makes me feel quite at home. There's nothing artificial, no tactics, not a trace of obsequiousness. Genie wears hardly any make-up, she usually dresses casually, discreetly, and prefers blue, the colour of her eyes. Her open face, intelligent eyes and warm smile invite me to get to know her better.

When I do, I meet an intelligent, cultivated and, above all, consistent woman, who knew very early on what sort of life she was going to follow. Although she doesn't seem the maternal type, she corresponds to that traditional cliché. She knows that, and it's what she wants. Her self-image as housewife and mother includes a pronounced level of social commitment. It wasn't until the early nineties that she gave up some of her voluntary positions: for example, with the American Red Cross, the Suffolk County Child Development Agency, which deals with seriously disabled children, and United Way, one of the leading American charity organizations.

There was no room left for the pursuit of a profession. Her social commitment was a task in itself, and her family was, and remains, the centre of her life: above all Walter, whom she loves and for whom she would walk through fire, but also their children, Bill, Tom, Dana and John. The sons, incidentally, have a rather conflictual relationship with their famous uncle. Like many of their generation they have a critical outlook on many things associated with his name – Vietnam, Cambodia or Chile, for example. In this regard, their father keeps his own counsel, but when necessary defends his brother in debates at home. That's his principle within the family, just as it is in public.

Genie not only describes him as charming, polite and obliging, she also says that he is extremely correct and a man of great integrity. I can only confirm this. The quality accords with his elegantly reticent manner. The grand public appearances that

The woman at Walter's side: Genie Kissinger during the interview at the Colorado ranch, August 2004.

his brother Henry likes to stage are not Walter's thing, although he still has various offices and, among other things, runs the family foundation, along with Genie. He doesn't make use of his honorary doctorate.

Walter makes no secret of his hobbies, which he still pursues today: riding, motorbikes and deep-sea diving. He flew his own plane at an early age. When he is on the ranch, the eighty-year-old spends up to four hours a day in the saddle. Concentrated sport – riding, in his case – is both a distraction and a way of relaxing.

Horses are his passion. Walter owns an imposing herd of Arab thoroughbreds and rides – what else? – the lead stallion. Gofer, a proud black horse, is also at the centre of our first filming day, on which we are spoiled with wonderful weather. After fog and downpours we have a steely blue sky, a blazing sun, and glittering fresh snow on the peaks – a sensation in August and a breathtaking backdrop for our external shots. Luck is always part of it.

Inside, I notice that there are also strange aspects to Walter's life on the ranch. We shouldn't be surprised that a music-lover with no interest in the modern stuff should prefer the great German composers, Mozart, Beethoven, Schubert or Brahms. But then, on the first evening, after we have visited his collection of saddles and rifles, when we sit down to dinner in the comfortable sitting room, German marching music rings out in the background. Clearly Walter has put it on specially for this occasion, and when Genie irritably asks after a while what kind of peculiar music this is and whether he couldn't possibly choose something else, he opts for the German national anthem.

This in turn prompts Walter to ask if it is still the anthem of the Germans. He is concerned by a lot of things this evening: what do we Germans think of the Nazi period today? How do we react to this legacy from our parents? It's a difficult and very

Proud and free: Walter Kissinger on 'Gofer', the leading stallion of his Arabian herd, inspects his property in Colorado, August 2004.

'Can we stop the camera?' On the terrace of his ranch in Colorado: Walter Kissinger in conversation about the fate of his family, August 2004.

21

personal conversation. And in this way, step by step, we approach the theme of the interview.

It takes place on the terrace. The weather is still beautiful. Ideal conditions for a relaxed conversation, in fact, so I begin the interview with the here and now, asking him about the ranch and the horses. And the closer we edge towards his childhood and youth, the more nervous and monosyllabic Walter becomes. Even his poor cat, which he has enticed on to his lap, and he is now practically kneading with his hands, can't calm him.

Then, when Walter, visibly moved, asks for the camera to be turned off and goes into the house, I am not sure he'll come back. At least I am allowed to include this scene of shattering speechlessness in the film. You get the sense that he put this chapter of his life behind him long ago. Now the images are rising up in front of him, and gradually the story of Heinz and Walter Kissinger assumes an outline for me, too.

The story of Heinz and Walter

Part One: The Expulsion

You don't often get days like these, even in a long and far from uneventful life. Almost ninety years lie behind the man who, on that sunny but cold December day in 1975, addressed the dignitaries and guests of honour of the city of Fürth, in a firm voice, yet visibly moved. Louis Kissinger was not born in Fürth. But he had spent the 'major part' of his German life there: 'It was here that I founded my family, here that our two sons were born, here that I spent the happiest years of my working life.'

Until the Nazis came. Then Louis Kissinger, his wife Paula and their two sons, Heinz and Walter, were forced to leave the city. That was almost forty years ago now, half a lifetime. Louis Kissinger had found a new home in the United States a long time ago. That 'great country' didn't just give the German exile 'a fresh opportunity', it also opened up 'a new future' for his sons.

And yet the city whose representatives he was now addressing in their mother tongue, in a local accent that is impossible to ignore, has always 'been close to his heart'. This 'great esteem' for Fürth lies in its remarkable history. Louis Kissinger studied it when he was very young, and there is a strong line of tradition that was crucial in leading him to move to Fürth and founding his family there: 'While intolerance and prejudice predominated in many German cities in past centuries, in Fürth the different faiths lived together in harmony.'

The place where the Pegnitz and the Rednitz flow together to form the Regnitz, and whose existence is first documented in 1007, has something of a chequered past. The Thirty Years War in particular left deep traces. That great disaster of European history arose out of the religious divisions of the time. The war was correspondingly grim. A rather local event, the Bohemian uprising, developed from 1618 onwards into a European power struggle, fought out entirely in the territory of the Holy Roman Empire, leading to terrible losses and huge destruction. Bavaria lost more than a third of its population. Countless towns were razed to the ground, including Fürth.

Here and in Nuremberg the Swedish king Gustavus Adolphus set up camp in July 1632, until, a few weeks later, not far from the city walls, in the shadow of the derelict fortress, the Alte Veste, he was forced to retreat by the army of the German-Roman emperor, Ferdinand II. Albrecht Wenzel Eusebius von Wallenstein, the emperor's most important general, commanded the mostly Bavarian troops. Two years later, passing Croatian troops demolished the city, apart from a few houses. The story of the 'Swedish drink', a form of torture that involved pouring large amounts of liquid manure or similar substances into the victim, was still told when Heinz and Walter Kissinger sat at their school desks.

After that the situation calmed down a little, even though various rulers went on struggling for power in Fürth. Until 1792 the city was jointly ruled by the margraves of Ansbach, the diocese of Bamberg, and the city of Nuremberg. Then Fürth fell to Prussia for a few years, before becoming part of Bavaria, after which it received official city status, and took charge of its own city administration from 1818 onwards. Prussian rule had not lasted long, but it left traces behind: it was then that the Franconian market town received the first stimulus for the industrialization that allowed it to step out of the shadow of its powerful neighbour, Nuremberg. In 1835, when the first stretch of German railway line opened between the two cities, the name of Fürth became known far and wide.

From that time until the outbreak of the First World War, Fürth enjoyed its heyday. This is borne out by the Rathaus, built in the Italian style before the middle of the century, with its 180-foot-high tower modelled on the Palazzo Vecchio in Florence; the cast-iron monumental fountain in front of the railway station, inaugurated in 1890; and the Stadttheater, which opened in 1902. The dynamic development of the city was reflected in its population growth, which soared from the 1880s onwards. Among the new citizens were quite a few who would go on to make a name for themselves both inside and outside the city walls – politicians and businessmen, authors and publishers.

Leopold Ullstein, for example, who was born here in 1823 and later laid the foundations of a major book and newspaper empire, or Jakob Wassermann, born in 1873, who was one of the most popular authors in the German-speaking world. Fürth could even be said to be the cradle of the future German economic miracle. In 1895, Gustav Schickedanz, the founder of the Quelle mail-order company, also based in Fürth, was born here. A hundred years later, Henry Kissinger, born in the city as Heinz and raised there, and now one of its most famous sons, delivered the official address.

The list of famous sons of the city of Fürth also includes Ludwig Erhard, who came into the world two years after Gustav Schickedanz, in February 1897. Wounded in the First World War, he was unable to take over his parents' linen-goods shop on Sternstrasse, which now bears his name, and initially tried his hand at a career in science. No one could have predicted that this would eventually lead to his becoming Chancellor of West Germany.

When Ludwig Erhard was growing up in Fürth at the turn of the twentieth century, the city was not only the seat of a district authority and a regional and county court. It was also home to a pensions office and a custom house, a branch of the Reichsbank, an agency of the Bayerische Notenbank, and a district committee for trade and business. These were all in great demand in Fürth at the time.

The chief commodities produced in the city were the so-called 'Nuremberg goods.' Eighty factories specialized in the production of mirrors alone. Alongside this, there were manufacturers of gold leaf and metal foils, bronze and bronze paints, steel spectacles and optical instruments, furniture and cardboard packing, mechanical engineers, belt-makers, turners and bookbinders. The trading houses of Fürth maintained contact with all parts of the world; ten banking and trading houses ensured a decent turnover, and every year the eleven-day St Michael's Fair brought powerful customers and interested parties to the city.

At the same time, Fürth could not really be described as a metropolis. The city lies in the shadow of Nuremberg, only a few miles away, with its imposing castle and almost 150,000 inhabitants. In 1890 the population of Fürth was only a third of that. But one group was represented almost as strongly as it was in Nuremberg. Just under 3,200 Jews, or 'Israelites', as they were called at the time, lived on the river Regnitz in 1890.

That was no coincidence, because in the history of the German Jews – or, at least, the Bavarian Jews – Fürth occupies a unique position. Leaving aside the confusions of the Thirty Years War, the Jews, who had, with interruptions, lived in Fürth since 1440, were spared persecution and expulsion for centuries. That was partly why the events that followed the Nazis' assumption of power came as such an unimaginable, profoundly shocking experience for them; throughout the whole of his life a man like Louis Kissinger couldn't really understand how it could have come to this, here of all places.

Because for German Jews, Fürth had never been a place of expulsion, but always a place of refuge. The city's Jewish community came into being in the first half of the sixteenth century, at a time when Jews often had to leave other cities and territories. Many of them found a place to stay in Fürth, including Jews from neighbouring Nuremberg, which had expelled them in 1499.

So Fürth soon took Nuremberg's place as a flourishing centre of Bavarian Jewry. The city and its Jewish community profited from the lasting political rivalry of the lords of Nuremberg, Bamberg and Ansbach. The margrave of Ansbach allowed two Jews to settle in Fürth for the first time in 1528. In those days such privileges were not to be had for free. Annual statements of account and generous financial sacrifices were the price that the Jews of Fürth had to pay for their independence. At least that meant they were spared the Ansbach expulsion mandate of 1560, and until well into the eighteenth century they survived all the attempts of Nuremberg city council to get rid of their bothersome Jewish competition in Fürth.

Two hundred Jews lived in Fürth in 1582, and, as the community owed its existence to expulsion, over the coming decades and centuries they profited not least from the influx of their exiled co-religionists. In 1670, for example, part of the Jewish community expelled from Vienna found its new home there. In the early nineteenth century, when Fürth became part of Bavaria and assumed city status, nearly two and a half thousand Jews lived there. Most of them enjoyed full community rights.

Apart from settlement rights, these included the active and passive right to elect the mayor. They were also granted permission to resolve legal matters amongst themselves, to exercise police powers and criminal law, and even to call upon the legal assistance of the Christian authorities. Most importantly, however, the right to self-administration and religious worship was unlimited. Since the early nineteenth century, Jews had sat as magistrates and as members of the district council, played an important part in the city's business life, and acted as generous benefactors.

Fürth, moreover, developed into a centre of rabbinical

teaching and Jewish culture. The famous Yeshivah, Fürth's Talmudic college, held its own against the Talmudic schools in Hamburg and Frankfurt. Until it was closed by the Bavarian authorities in 1824, it attracted Jews from all over Germany, including, for example, Mayer Amschel Rothschild, the founder of the banking dynasty, and introduced them to the study and interpretation of its post-biblical teachings. Much of this was still evident in the early years of the twentieth century. Small wonder that Fürth still attracted young, cultured Jews – among them Louis Kissinger.

Since 1999 a museum in Fürth has recalled the rich Jewish history of the city and the surrounding area. The building stands on Königstrasse and is part of an ensemble of similar buildings with sandstone facades and mansard roofs, built after the Thirty Years War in the wake of the eastward extension of the city by affluent Jewish businessmen. At number eighty-nine, which is now the museum, stucco ceilings and baroque door fittings testify to the social standing of the people who lived there; the tabernacle, the mikvah – the ritual bath in the cellar – and traces of the mesusah – the capsule containing the profession of the Jewish faith fastened to the right doorpost – are reminders that Jews lived here. Such traces are distributed all over the city.

However, Jewish Fürth, strictly speaking, consisted of two parallel worlds. Most of the Jewish population had belonged to the enlightened, liberal wing of Judaism since the mid-nineteenth century. Many showed tendencies towards assimilation, which sometimes led to baptism and often to marriage with non-Jewish men, or, even more often, non-Jewish women. The focus of the enlightened Fürth Jews was the main synagogue, built in 1617. It was attended, however, less frequently than the four subsidiary synagogues. These were grouped around the schoolyard and were the ones that the city's Orthodox Jews attended, including the teacher Louis Kissinger, with his sons Heinz and Walter.

The difference between the two worlds was not restricted to questions of philosophy and religion, it was also reflected in social status and access to education. The more affluent Jewish families, who chiefly belonged to the liberal wing, sent their children to the city Gymnasium, the grammar school. On the other hand, the children of the Orthodox Jews attended the Jewish Realschule. For them, the Gymnasium was out of the question because pupils there had to write on Saturdays, which is forbidden to Orthodox Jews.

The fact that Louis Kissinger taught at an institution of this kind, the city girls' grammar school, the Mädchenlyzeum, even though he was a strictly observant Jew, is remarkable. But if it had been up to him and his wife, his sons would also have attended the city Gymnasium. That wasn't to happen, however, because the National Socialists reduced the number of Jews permitted at public schools to a vanishingly small percentage, practically forbidding them access. So Heinz and Walter Kissinger sat at desks in the Jewish Realschule on Blumenstrasse, where, following its foundation in 1862, it had moved into a severely classical building in 1869.

Following Blumenstrasse to the north-west, and turning into Theaterstrasse, one comes to the former Jewish hospital, which was rebuilt in 1846. For Jews, the treatment of the sick is a religious obligation. In 1943 this institution was closed by the Nazis. After the end of the war, the first members of the newly founded Jewish religious community were lodged here. Today the building is used as a residential home. Diagonally opposite, at 23 Mathildenstrasse, on the corner with Theaterstrasse, stands the house where Heinz Kissinger was born. Here, in the immediate vicinity of the Jewish schoolyard and the synagogues that surrounded it, Louis Kissinger and his wife lived in a small flat with a balcony on the first floor. When, a year later, they moved to 5 Marienstrasse, where Walter was born shortly afterwards, they would remain in this same Jewish quarter.

The Jewish orphanage was in this part of town, too. Founded in 1763, it was the first of its kind in Germany. Children from all over the country were admitted to it, and Louis Kissinger sometimes taught there, in the afternoons and for free. During the night of the Reich pogrom the mob stormed the building, which also contained a synagogue, and destroyed the interior furnishings. In March 1942 thirty-three Jewish children were deported from here to Izbica and murdered, along with the director of the orphanage, Dr Isaak Hallemann, who had stayed for the sake of the children. The building now houses the synagogue of the city's Jewish religious community.

Fürth's Jewish community was never able to regain its former greatness. By the night of 8 November 1938, when the city's synagogues and other institutions of Jewish life were destroyed, many Jews had already left their city, many of them literally at the last minute. They included the family of the teacher Louis Kissinger. He could not have imagined that he would have to flee his city and country because he was a Jew; but even in the years when he was growing up there had been the initial signs of difficult times ahead.

When Louis Kissinger was born in February 1887 things were calm only on the surface. The German imperial Reich had just turned sixteen, and had long since established itself as one of the leading states of Europe and the world. On the foundation of the Reich, Germany had become, after Russia, the largest territorial state and the most populous nation on the European continent; and following three wars, fought quickly and successfully, the Reich was the most successful military power of its day. Economically Germany was well on the way to overtaking most of its neighbours; it was in the front line in terms of culture and the sciences, and had even been active as a colonial power since the 1880s.

The Germans must have seemed, on the surface, a confident, cosmopolitan, forward-looking people. But on closer inspection it became apparent that their confidence was short-lived, that much of it was a defiant act, and that beneath the surface things were fermenting. In fact, the Germans had become deeply pessimistic and did not believe there were good times ahead. The prime cause of this state of mind was economic development. Not that it was going downhill; it was more that it was no longer going uphill, or at least not at the rate that had followed the unification of the Reich, which had set the standard.

As early as 1873 disillusionment had set in, which has gone down in history as the 'Gründerkrach', the 'founders' crash'. From that time on, the national economy proceeded at a rather more leisurely pace. We cannot talk of an economic crisis in the strict sense of the word, yet that was how the Germans interpreted it, and soon the phrase 'Great Depression' was doing the rounds. It was more a diffuse feeling than a realistic reaction to the state of the economy.

What is surprising is the fact that this did not change even in 1896, when the less spectacular years gave way to a boom period which continued right up until the beginning of the First World War. The widespread sense of crisis that had taken root, above all in the educated and property-owning classes, did not ease at all. And because in times of actual or supposed crisis people seek scapegoats, now, in the 1870s, the Jews entered the sights of the prophets of economic doom.

The crisis that followed the Gründerkrach not only represented the birth of modern anti-Semitism, it actually gave it its name. The term first appeared in 1879. From its beginnings, this 'anti-Semitism' concealed an attempt to give the most diffuse prejudices a foundation and thus a legitimacy. Its protagonists included, among others, Adolf Stöcker. 'No people', the Berlin court and cathedral preacher told his audience in 1882, 'suffers so much from the oppressive influence of Jewry as the German people ... If we do not shake off this yoke, our entire future will be in danger ... Therefore let it resound from this hall to the whole country: Germany, Christian people, bestir yourselves, wake up!'

A simple but effective strategy: by attributing to the Jews a dominant position in the cultural, political, and, not least, the economic life of the Reich, it gave visible and identifiable form to those it would hold chiefly responsible for the poverty of the years of crisis.

In fact, it was not simply a question of preventing the legal and political equality of the Jews, it was a matter of turning the clock back. It was still scarcely possible for Jews to carve a career for themselves in the civil service. The doors to leading positions in the bureaucracy, the diplomatic service and the military were largely closed to them; in the German Reich there was not a single Jewish career officer. Yet the Jews were leaving the social margins and were to a great extent integrated. From that point of view, anti-Semitism was a reaction against their long-standing assimilation in many areas of life.

In order to mobilize society in support of its goals, to give anti-Semitism a mass foundation, the movement entered into an explosive alliance with nationalism: the Jews represented everything that was damaging to the nation. This both required and justified the struggle against them. The agitation was unsuccessful at first. If we bear in mind that the anti-Semitic movement had powerful organizations on its side, such as the German Student Body, the Landlords' Association, and the many members of the Pan-German Union, it received surprisingly little response. From the political elite of the Reich to the working classes, who were at the time becoming a serious force in German society, it was broadly met with rejection or indifference. At the parliamentary level, organized anti-Semitism had practically ceased to exist by the outbreak of the war.

Still, the Jews reacted, and in 1893 set up the Central Association of German Citizens of Jewish Faith. Louis Kissinger himself became a member. The association's goals included unlimited equality, not least in the civil service, and the defeat of anti-Semitism, the strongholds of which lay in those places where the economic crisis had, actually or supposedly, shown its face particularly clearly, not least in the provinces. On the other hand, large parts of the country, including many cities, remained largely untouched by the anti-Semitic agitation.

Particularly in cities such as Fürth, where Jews and Christians had lived together for centuries, the turn of the century wave of anti-Semitism passed almost without a trace. Louis Kissinger moved to the city in 1905.

The Kissingers had had their roots in Franconia for generations. Most of the male members of the family had made their living as teachers. As so-called *Judenlehrer* or Jewish teachers, they taught only Jewish children in the religious communities. Louis's great-grandfather, born in Kleinebstadt around 1760, with the name Meyer Loeb, had worked as a teacher in Bad Kissingen and Rödelsee. He was also the one who, with reference to the town of Bad Kissingen, took the surname of Kissinger. In doing so, he was complying with the terms of the Bavarian Jewish Edict – which was passed in 1813 but did not come into effect in some communities, such as Fürth, until 1820 – which obliged Jews to take family names.

Meyer's second wife, the sister of his first, also came from Kissingen. Meyer Loeb Kissinger's first wife, née Marianne David-Stahl, born in 1783, had died in childbirth on 1 May 1812; of her two surviving children only one had descendants. After Marianne's death, Meyer Loeb Kissinger married her sister, Schoenlein David- Stahl. Of their many children, only one seems to have survived, Abraham Kissinger, born in Rödelsee on 29 October 1818.

Abraham Kissinger, a successful weaver and trader, decided that all his sons would follow the teaching profession, since this would ensure that they had a secure income. Following their father's wish, the four sons, Joseph, Maier, Simon and David Kissinger, left Rödelsee and worked in neighbouring villages as Jewish teachers. As there were no rabbis in most of these little places, they also worked as prayer leaders for the Jewish communities. In this way, David Kissinger, born on 13 June 1860, came to Ermershausen, and became cantor and teacher of religion to the Jewish community there.

Jews had lived in that village in Lower Franconia, first documented in 1049, since their expulsion from the cities in the fifteenth and sixteenth centuries. In the early nineteenth century, of just 450 inhabitants of Ermershausen almost a hundred professed the Jewish faith. That had changed by the end of the century, because many Jews left after they were granted permission to live anywhere they wanted, in 1861; between 1865 and 1881 alone, forty-one Jewish inhabitants moved away from Ermershausen.

David Kissinger, on the other hand, resisted the trend and stayed, because he wanted to look after the shrinking community and because he had lost his heart to a woman from Ermershausen. Shortly after his arrival he had met Karolina Zeilberger, three days younger than he was, and he soon asked for her hand in marriage. They were a pretty couple: dark-haired Karolina, with a full face beneath a smart fringe, big eyes, shapely nose and full lips; and imposing David, who wore a full beard – later, a trimmed goatee – always with a faint smile playing round his lips, and unimaginable without his hat and metal-rimmed glasses.

Before they could marry, David had to apply for citizenship in Ermershausen, as the law decreed. Fortunately, Lina, as she

Pious and cultured: David Kissinger, the father of Louis and grandfather of Henry and Walter Kissinger.

A good catch: Karolina 'Lina' Zeilberger, David Kissinger's wife, was attractive and wealthy.

was known, was the daughter of a wealthy farmer, who gave her a dowry of 10,000 gold marks. In view of such prospects, the authorities in Ermershausen were most obliging: on 13 July 1884, David Kissinger was granted citizenship, and immediately afterwards he married Karolina Zeilberger.

The marriage produced seven children: Jenny, who died of pneumonia at the age of just six, Ida, Selma, Fanny, Karl, Arno and Louis. On 2 February 1887, Louis Kissinger was born, the second oldest child of David and Lina. From what we know, the boy had a carefree childhood and youth in Ermershausen. That was also partly due to his father's job, which meant that he was completely integrated into village life. His penchant for engaging in philosophical discussions on his walks through the vineyards of the Main region suggests not a withdrawn, introverted person, but a communicative, cosmopolitan character.

David Kissinger was a cheerful man with a pronounced sense of humour. Every Saturday evening after the end of Shabbas, Rabbi David Kissinger met up with the tailor, the cobbler and the landlord in the village pub for a bibulous and jovial game of cards. Nominally David Kissinger belonged to the Orthodox community, but his whole lifestyle suggested that he was a man of the modern age – a man of the twentieth century, one might say. After the turn of the century, for example, the Kissingers had their own telephone line, which in those days was a sign of progress and affluence.

In the autumn of his own life, his son Louis spoke with respect of the high standing his father had enjoyed among the people of Ermershausen. That was part of the reason why the son wanted to tread in his father's footsteps, and had decided early on to work as a teacher. But Louis broke with family tradition by opting to work not as a Judenlehrer, but as a teacher in the public school system.

*

We don't know when he made that decision. But we do know that the journey there was long and tortuous. First, the ambitious young man from Ermershausen had to finish his education. In 1900 we find the thirteen-year-old at the Königliche Präparandenschule Arnstein. In mid-July the following year his teachers gave a clear and entirely positive assessment of their pupil, who was 'among the best in the class'.

'With his many mental aptitudes,' his annual report reads, 'his praiseworthy homework, along with eagerness and attentiveness in class, in all respects he has made his teachers most satisfied. His religious, moral and disciplinary attitude has been entirely blameless.' This is reflected in his marks. Admittedly in drawing and writing he was only 'average', but his achievements in the German language and in music were 'good', and in religious education, arithmetic, geography, history and natural history 'very good'. And in this spirit he quickly and successfully left his schooldays behind.

Aspiring teacher Louis Kissinger was eighteen when he first applied for a teaching post. The Vereinigte Heberleinsche and Arnsteinsche Institut was founded by Simon Geiershofer in 1848 as a private institution for girls, and merged in 1883 with the Heberleinsche Töchterschule, also a private foundation. It was Fürth's first private secondary school for girls. Originally founded for the daughters of Jewish families, since the turn of the century about half of the pupils had been of the Christian faith, most of them Protestant. The school had only been in existence for sixty years when, after the city Mädchenlyzeum on Tannenstrasse began teaching, the private institution closed its doors at the end of June 1907.

Until that date, Louis Kissinger held his first teaching post there. At the beginning of November 1905 the headmaster of the Heberleinsche and Arnsteinsche Höhere Mädchenschule allowed the aspiring teacher to be 'brought in' to give up to five lessons a week of Jewish religious instruction to the youngest classes – a modest teaching load, but it was a start. The young teacher was able to show what he was capable of doing, and that proved to be a great deal.

In March 1906, after an unannounced inspection, the rabbinate pronounced an extremely favourable result: 'I am now happy to say', the report to the headmaster reads, 'that I was completely satisfied by the thorough extraordinary inspection that I carried out. In the interest of the school I recommend as a matter of urgency that for this year, in this combined department, no further changes to the teaching staff should be undertaken, all the more so in that Herr Kissinger seems to catch the right tone in his dealings with his pupils.'

The headmaster seemed to make a similarly positive judgement when he gave the teacher his reference six months later, on 18 September 1906: 'Herr L.K.', it says, 'has worked since the beginning of the 1905 school year at the school of the undersigned as teacher to the third and fourth classes. The undersigned testifies most precisely that this relatively very young teacher proved himself at the very start of his professional activity to be an unusually industrious, capable and active pedagogue, and that since then he has shown himself to be extremely conscientious, punctual and responsible in every respect, and with his enjoyment of the work and love of the children has achieved the most excellent educational results.'

Louis Kissinger had found his vocation. He was not even twenty and his employers were already testifying to the very qualities in this impassioned pedagogue that his pupils would remember in their old age. Yet he was just at the beginning of a long life, professionally as well as privately. Where his 'private life' was concerned, the headmaster of his first school described it as 'most praiseworthy'. Of course, the young teacher lived at first as a lodger, starting with a room on Theaterstrasse. After then lodging for some time with the master baker Berle Oppenheimer on Hirschenstrasse, from the beginning of

December 1908 he took a room at 42 Schwabacherstrasse.

By now Louis Kissinger was teaching at the private Heckmannschule, founded in 1897. He had probably taken the new job after the Heberleinsche und Arnsteinsche Höhere Mädchenschule was forced to close. At any rate, on 20 September 1909 he sat the employment exam. He was now teaching for an annual income of 1000 Reichsmarks – boys this time, because the Heckmannschule was for boys alone.

The pupils were initially surprised, and looked with some scepticism at the twenty-two-year-old standing in front of them who wanted to be their teacher. But they soon noticed that this was someone, young or not, who wanted, with passion, tenacity and talent, to give them something to take on life's journey. Until 1919 Louis Kissinger taught German, maths, science and modern languages – at first only a combined first and second class, finally four classes a day. But there were interruptions.

For Louis Kissinger, the years between 1909 and 1919 were a phase of searching, orientation and, of course, uncertainty. The war that cast a spell first over Europe and then over the whole world after the summer of 1914, and when it came to an end in 1918 was described by contemporaries as a world war, left no one untouched – not even those who, like the teacher, or student teacher, Louis Kissinger, were not conscripted for military service. Even before the outbreak of war his career had revealed attempts to find new professional horizons. He wanted to remain a teacher; but Louis Kissinger, like most people of his age, was an ambitious man. He wanted to get to the top, he wanted a better job and with it a higher salary. There were two ways of getting there. Either he would have to look for a new post calling for similar qualifications, or he would have to work on those qualifications and so rise through the government service. Over the next few years Louis Kissinger did both.

He repeatedly applied for teaching posts outside of Fürth. In 1910 his application to the Israelitische Präparandenschule

Talmud-Thora in Burgpreppach was successful, but he evidently rejected the post. At least, in the middle of August 1910 the school sent the applicant his documents back, to Ermershausen, where Louis Kissinger could still be contacted, and where he clearly lived during the school holidays. In the summer of 1918 he was successful in his application for a post in Beuthen in Upper Silesia; for work 'chiefly teaching religious instruction, Hebrew and related subjects in the Jewish Volkschule, Gymnasium, Realgymnasium and Lyzeum', Louis Kissinger was offered an annual starting salary of 4000 Reichsmarks, as well as a living allowance.

Why he applied to Upper Silesia, and then turned down the job, is uncertain. Perhaps he wanted to improve at the Heckmannschule. But he would appear not to have intended his application to be taken altogether seriously, because a year earlier he had taken the second path and started work on his own training. On 29 April 1917, Louis, now thirty years old, applied to the Royal Bavarian State Ministry of the Interior for Church and School Matters to sit the school-leaving examination, and was allocated to the Königliche Realgymnasium in Nuremberg 'to sit the exam'.

Louis Kissinger wanted to teach at a public school, in Fürth, which was now his home. On 20 November 1917, Nuremberg city council granted him the citizenship he had applied for, and five weeks before that he had already begun his studies at Erlangen, the nearest university. From the winter semester of 1917–18 until the winter semester of 1922–3, with a few interruptions, he studied first economics, then philosophy, also taking an interest in a wide range of other subjects.

On 10 April 1919 he was awarded his first university qualification. His school exams and studies had achieved their goal. In the post-war period, with its shortage of teachers, this qualification was quite enough for a post in the public service. In the 1919–20 annual report of the Städtische Höhere Mädchenschule

Fürth, Louis Kissinger, who had been living on Nürnberger Strasse since the beginning of November 1918, first appears as a senior master (Hauptlehrer) of German, arithmetic, science and modern languages. The Lyzeum, which had since its inception incorporated a city business school for girls, had enjoyed great popularity with the citizens of Fürth right from the beginning. Such was the demand that in 1909, two years after it had opened, the Höhere Töchterschule had to build a second schoolhouse on Tannenstrasse.

So it was here, in what is now the Helene-Lange-Gymnasium, that Louis Kissinger was permanently employed by a government resolution of 3 March 1920, and from 1921 onwards as a senior master. His dream of teaching in a public institution was finally a reality. Until the Nazis prevented him from practising his profession, he stayed with the school. He was soon as well respected at his new workplace as he had been at his old one. He usually came into the classroom with a book under his arm, stepped up to his lectern with a lively, almost skipping gait, and called out to his class to 'Sit, sit!' – because, of course, the class would have stood up as soon as their teacher appeared in the doorway.

Louis Kissinger was by now in his mid-thirties and an attractive man, of medium height, with symmetrical features, striking ears, slightly wavy, almost curly, combed-back hair, and a thin moustache. He was always correctly dressed and wore a bow tie – later, an ordinary tie – and more often than not a three-piece suit. His pupils called him 'Kissus', and some girls still admit, even as elderly women, that they were secretly in love with him.

That was because of his imposing appearance, and the way the teacher approached his girl pupils. One of them later spoke of the appearance of Louis Kissinger. When he asked her, in

Surrounded by admirers: Louis Kissinger, known as 'Kissus', on an outing with his girl pupils in Fürth.

their very first class, about logarithms, and she had to give in, the new teacher said, 'Girl, when I was your age I didn't know that either. All these things have to be learnt.' It was passion that drove him as a teacher, and that also meant that he was patient, and when his pupils didn't understand things straight-away he would explain them all over again.

Of course, the boys quickly spotted his weaknesses. Louis Kissinger wasn't a particularly strict teacher; he did have a cane at the ready, as teachers did in those days, but he hardly ever used it. As a result, the boys liked to play tricks on him. Stories still circulate among his former pupils today. For example, the boys once undid the screws of the board in front of the washbasin on which their teacher was in the habit of leaning, and needless to say, achieved the desired effect: the drenched 'Kissus' had to interrupt his class to go home and change. Word soon got round that on Saturdays Louis Kissinger was an easy victim: because of Shabbas, he wasn't allowed to write, so he couldn't make any entries in the class-book.

But Kissinger had too good a reputation as a teacher to be damaged by such incidents. He could teach you a few things, not least the German language. His pupils were struck by the fact that he spoke quite a pure form of German, with a slight Franconian accent, but not with the harsh intonation that one tends to hear in Fürth. He was particularly fond of poetry, and he especially loved teaching German poems. Even today, his former pupils, and also his sons, elderly though they are, can still recite the poems of Goethe or Heine by heart.

Henry Kissinger, the elder of the two, sometimes even does so in public, as he did, for example, in January 1999 when friends and colleagues of Helmut Schmidt celebrated the former Chancellor's eightieth birthday in the Thalia Theater in Hamburg. This time the speaker did not discuss problems of global politics, but instead recited two poems that his father had taught him: Goethe's 'The Eagle and the Dove' and Heine's

'Where Now?' And when Henry, who had had to leave Germany as Heinz a good sixty years previously, recited this poem, many people had the feeling that he was talking about himself and his father:

> *Whither now? My foolish feet*
> *Like to head for Germany;*
> *But my reason shakes its head,*
> *Seems to say sagaciously:*
>
> *'Though the war is over now,*
> *Martial law reigns as before,*
> *And your pen has penned, they say*
> *Executables galore.*
>
> *I'm no hero, and I'd find it*
> *Quite unpleasant to be shot,*
> *Lacking all the histrionics*
> *So essential to that lot.*
>
> *I would like to go to England,*
> *Were it not for colliery damps*
> *And the English – just their fragrance*
> *Gives me nausea and cramps.*
>
> *Now and then in thoughts I travel*
> *To America, my sights*
> *On that spacious freedom stable*
> *Filled with louts of equal rights.*
>
> *But I'm fearful of a land*
> *Where the men are 'baccy-chawers*
> *Where they bowl without a king,*
> *And ignore the cuspidors.*

Russia now, that handsome realm,
Might agree with me, who knows,
But I might not gladly bear
Being flogged in winter snows.

Woefully I gaze aloft,
Where a thousand starlets glitter,
But my own good fortune's star
I find nowhere in that litter.

Haply it has gone astray,
In these labyrinthine blazes,
Just as I have lost my way
Here in these terrestrial mazes.'

The school was Louis Kissinger's life, so it was no coincidence that it was there that he also met the love of his life. When visiting a friend and colleague he met the young Paula Stern. They already knew each other slightly, because Paula had graduated from the school at which Louis now taught. He hadn't taught her, but he knew the marks she had received in her graduation exam, and was impressed by them.

The two of them could hardly have been more different: he was shy and introverted, she sparkling by nature and full of the joys of life. Still, that evening Louis overcame his shyness and walked Paula to her aunt's house. Neither of them could have guessed at the time that this was to be the start of a journey that would last for over half a century and take them through the highs and lows of their life together.

Paula Stern was born on 25 February 1901, at ten o'clock in the morning, in Leutershausen in Franconia. Her parents, Falk and Peppi Stern, had married in Ansbach in November 1898. They were among the sixty-two Jewish men, women and children still living in Leutershausen around 1900. The others – as was

47

the case in Ermershausen, Louis Kissinger's birthplace – had either emigrated or, since they had been granted freedom of residence, moved to larger towns in search of better and more diverse prospects.

Leutershausen, first documented in the year 1000, is a small town between Ansbach and Rothenburg ob der Tauber, right on the river Altmühl. The settlement was probably founded in the wake of the first wave of Franconian land development in the seventh and eighth centuries. There are references to Jewish inhabitants from the fifteenth century, the time when most Bavarian and Franconian cities were expelling Jews. But even in Leutershausen the immigrants were not always welcome: occasional acts of violence made life difficult for them, and Jews wishing to move there were not automatically granted permission by the city council.

When Paula was born, the Sterns had nothing to complain about. They lived well. Paula's father worked as a cattle-trader, a popular profession among Jews at the time, and he was successful and had a good income. Business was so good that in 1904 Falk Stern was able, along with his brother David, to buy the grand property at number eight Am Markt. It was in this spacious house, with its typical courtyard and pretty kitchen garden, that Paula grew up as a sheltered only child. She didn't miss having brothers and sisters, since a large circle of friends and attentive relations made sure she was well looked after. She was especially keen on visits to her grandmother's, and even in her old age her grandma's pancakes were among Paula's most cherished childhood memories.

Because Falk Stern did a lot of business with non-Jews, his family was more assimilated than, for example, the Kissinger family in Ermershausen. The Sterns participated eagerly and intensely in the social life of the town. For example, Falk Stern was a founder member of the local gymnastics club, and in December 1922 the voluntary fire service celebrated twenty-five

What does life have in store? Paula Stern, Henry and Walter's mother, was the only daughter of the Jewish cattle-trader Falk Stern from Leutershausen.

years of his membership. The Sterns were also welcome guests at parties given by non-Jewish families. Thus a photograph shows father Falk and his daughter Paula at a wedding thrown by the Keidels in Treisdorf.

Anti-Semitism, Paula recalled in her twilight years, was something that she neither saw nor sensed. Quite the contrary, as the daughter of the Jewish cattle-trader, she had been something special among the many peasant girls in Leutershausen. Paula was well liked, a stranger to self-doubt, proud of her Jewish origins.

At that time there was a synagogue in Leutershausen, where the twenty or so Jewish families gathered for prayer. Paula's parents were observant Jews; her father later spent fifteen years as chairman of the Jewish community until it was dissolved by the Nazis. In spite of their high level of assimilation, they adhered strictly to the religious regulations. They always ate at home, as the inns did not offer kosher food. Often, Jewish visitors came from elsewhere to have dinner with the Stern family. As a child, of course, Paula had hardly anything to do with the life of the community. But she did attend lessons in religious instruction every day after school, learnt Hebrew, and found out about the history of the Jewish people.

Her closest friend in her youth was a Protestant, Babette Hammerder, known as 'Babby'; six years older than Paula, her parents ran an agricultural machinery business in the town. Paula and Babby's friendship lasted all their lives. Paula attended the public school in Leutershausen along with Babby and the other village children. She was a good student. Above all, she liked to read, even in her free time. Her favourite reading matter included stories of the island of Mont Saint Michel and its famous Benedictine monastery. When Louis Kissinger went there with her after the Second World War, he fulfilled one of her youthful dreams. Paula was fully integrated and accepted at

Lifelong friendship: 'Babby' Hezner, née Hammerder (left) and Paula Kissinger, née Stern, in Leutershausen.

school, because she was spirited, and also because she was the daughter of a respected man.

As there was no secondary school in Leutershausen, when Paula was twelve her parents sent her to the Gymnasium in Fürth. The city was almost fifty miles away from Leutershausen, so Paula lodged in Fürth with her aunt, Berta Fleischmann. Berta was a sister of her father's, and ran a kosher butcher's and cook-shop in the city, on Hirschenstrasse. The flat was on the second floor of the building. Even if Paula Stern never felt as much at home in Fürth as she did in Leutershausen, she did have a good time there at first. Lessons, which were now the centre of her daily life, still gave her great pleasure.

But the situation soon changed – for the country, for the Stern family, and for their daughter Paula. Early in August 1914 even idyllic Leutershausen was split by the fault lines of global politics. When Austro-Hungary, the German Reich's closest and only reliable ally, became involved in a serious Balkan crisis after the murder in Sarajevo of the successor to the throne, the political and military leadership in Berlin showed unconditional solidarity. So, after weeks of mounting tension, almost overnight Germany found itself involved in another major European war. After the Reich decided to take firm action and declared war on Russia and France, on 1 and 3 August 1914, respectively, its troops marched into Belgium, and the British government responded by declaring war on Germany.

One of the German soldiers stationed in Belgium, for just under a year, was Paula's father. Falk Stern was fulfilling his duty. Many of his Jewish co-religionists volunteered for the army, because they had no doubt that Germany was engaged in a defensive war in which its very existence was at stake. Jewish organizations called upon their members to make themselves available to their homeland 'even beyond the call of duty'. In all, twelve thousand Jews ended up dying for their German fatherland.

But disillusionment soon set in among the ranks of Jewish soldiers. At the end of 1914, anti-Semitism showed its face at the front, and the longer the conflict dragged on, the more apparent, public and official it became. In October 1916, when the Prussian war minister ordered a statistical survey of the service of Jews in the war, they rightly saw this as a hidden form of administrative anti-Semitism. This 'Jew-counting', as it was called, was a slap in the face for patriotic German Jews, and it was also a signal. A year later, in October 1917, the newspaper of the Central Association of German Citizens of the Jewish Faith wrote with dark foreboding: 'We now face a war after the war.'

When Paula Stern looked back on her long life, she too saw the First World War as the crucial step towards anti-Semitism in Germany. She saw it at work in the conscription of her father. Paula could never forget that the German authorities called up Falk Stern even though he was forty-five years old – that and the fact that he was not given leave after the death of his wife.

Peppi Stern died on 4 July 1915 at the age of just forty-two. This was a turning point in her daughter's life; the loss of her beloved mother was a terrible blow. Paula was just fourteen years old and her mother's death marked the temporary end of her youth and her schooldays, which had just entered a new phase.

In December 1914 she had moved back to Fürth, returned to her lodgings with her uncle and aunt Fleischmann, and gone back to school. At first her mother's death did nothing to change the situation, because the 'businessman' Falk Stern had been called up for military service on 5 June 1915, a few weeks before his wife's death, and his daughter only returned to Leutershausen when her father was home on leave. But Falk Stern was only away at war for a year. Reassuring though this must have been for the motherless girl, the consequences were drastic. When her father was transferred to the locally based Landsturm-Infanterie-Ersatz Bataillon Nürnberg III B 16 and returned from Belgium, in the middle of May 1916, Paula had to take over the running of the household. Instead of studying mathematics or geography, she stood at the stove. It's impossible to say that she enjoyed it.

Now eighteen, although aware that her roots lay in Leutershausen, the enterprising and curious young woman was finding the little Franconian town very small and restricting. Paula was lonely and bored. Her father was strict; there was no question of her going out on her own in the evenings. Luckily, her friend Babby was there. She was by now going out with Karl Hezner, a very handsome rope-maker, who also ran a general goods store in Leutershausen, selling food, paints and chemical salts. Later he became a master examiner in rope-making, played an important part in the voluntary fire service, and, during the Second World War, was deployed as a fire-fighter in Nuremberg and Rothenberg.

As the couple were a little older than Paula, her father made an exception and sometimes allowed them to go out together in the evening. And if Falk Stern didn't allow that, then the two friends would pull Paula over the garden wall and go out dancing with her. These actions didn't go undiscovered, for Paula's step-mother became aware of them, but she said nothing. Her father had married thirty-one-year-old Fanny Walter, from Sugenheim in Ansbach, in April 1918, before the end of the war, and Paula had a good relationship with her stepmother.

By day, Paula and her two friends went on long rambles, sometimes going on trips to Dinkelsbühl or Rothenburg ob der Tauber. The young women also acted out plays or knitted and embroidered for their trousseaus under the direction of a needle-work teacher. Sporty Paula was a member of the gymnastics club and co-founder of a women's team, and she was still an enthusiastic reader. But in order to find books she had to travel to the nearest town, because there wasn't even a library in Leutershausen.

Nonetheless, books helped her to escape the narrow confines of the town, if at first only in her imagination. And because her stepmother soon took over the running of her new husband's household, Paula had the chance to travel and open up new horizons for herself. In the early 1920s she went to work as an au pair for a Jewish family in Halberstadt, in north Germany, looking after their four children. The factory owner's family took her in with open arms. They were very well-to-do, and Paula felt quite at home.

Back home in Franconia, the young woman finished her schooling in Fürth. Then, when she was invited to the home of one of her former teachers, she met the love of her life. Paula was just twenty, fourteen years younger than her future husband, and a very pretty girl. Louis was attracted by her spirit and her *joie de vivre*, but also by her cultivated, agile mind. Her dainty figure and regular features, with her big, radiant blue eyes, delicate lips and dark hair, usually combed back, all helped to cast a spell on her fiancé. On 28 July 1922, Paula Stern and Louis Kissinger said 'I do'.

Half a century later, when they celebrated their golden wedding in Switzerland, Louis reminded his family that it was generally seen as risky to marry the only daughter, but even riskier to marry the only child. And his wife was both, an only daughter and an only child. But fifty years previously he had made a 'clever and happy' decision: 'Paula was always a sensible, intelligent woman, and if I could turn the clock back I would marry Paula all over again.'

Louis was still a senior master, and his income was relatively small. Since he had only been permanently employed by the city of Fürth in 1919, he had hardly any savings, and those he

A journey shared: Louis Kissinger and Paula Stern, December 1921.

Paula Stern
Louis Kissinger

danken herzlichst für die ihnen anläßlich ih-
rer Verlobung erwiesene Aufmerksamkeit.

Leutershausen
Fürth

Dezember 1921

did have were eaten up by the inflation that reached unimaginable levels in 1922. Over the following year the German economy came close to collapse: unemployment was increasingly dramatically, and the exchange rate with the dollar rose from just under 18,000 Reichsmarks in January to 4.2 billion in November 1923, indicating the wretched state of the finances. Again at their golden wedding, Louis recalled the 'terrible inflation' that had wiped away everything they had saved.

These weren't really good times to form a lifelong bond and establish a family. However, the other hand the young couple, particularly the practically minded, energetic Paula, learned how to cope. First of all, they moved into a little apartment with a balcony at 23 Mathildenstrasse. The furniture was modest. After 1924 things started improving. The introduction of the Rentenmark on 15 November 1923 led to a general economic recovery, and also, on 1 September 1924, Louis Kissinger was promoted to the status of Oberlehrer, or senior master, with the status of a civil servant. Now the couple afford something better, and they moved into a more spacious apartment at 5 Marienstrasse.

Paula and Louis Kissinger were no longer alone. On 28 May 1923, the *Nordbayerische Zeitung* announced the 'happy birth of a boy': the previous day, on 27 May 1923, at half past five in the morning, Heinz Alfred came into the world. That this boy would one day go on to shape the fate of the world as Secretary of State of the most powerful country on earth was still written in the stars.

The Kissingers' first son was born at 23 Mathildenstrasse, with the help of a midwife. It was a gloomy May day, far too cold for the time of year. Heinz was a healthy, sturdy boy. A neighbour's girl who looked after the boy from time to time remembered him much later in life: 'A great fat devil with lots of hair.' Still, he didn't cry much. His proud father immediately called their friends the Rothschilds to tell them the happy news and invite them to the circumcision party.

Heinz's parents were profoundly religious, and that would never change. They lived in the part of Fürth populated by the city's Orthodox Jews, a good third of the three thousand Jews who lived in the city. For Louis, who joined the Orthodox community immediately after his arrival in Fürth, the religious education of his children was a matter very close to his heart. That applied not just to Heinz, but also to his second son, Walter Bernhard, who was born a year or so later, on 21 June 1924.

Needless to say, the two happy events in their teacher's life did not escape his pupils' notice. By the time Heinz was born, the class had held a collection so that they could give their 'Kissus' a present to celebrate the birth of his son and heir. But because there had been galloping inflation in the interim, the money had become worthless before the pupils could buy their teacher a gift. Gretlies Stäudtner was very unhappy about it, and tears flowed at home. Luckily, her mother knew what to do: she still had a few baby jackets. They were made for girls and had pink bows, but it was easy to thread in a blue one. So it was that Louis Kissinger received a present from his class for the birth of his son after all. And when Walter was born a year later there was a little jacket for him as well.

Of course, the teacher didn't expect a present from his pupils, especially with times as they were. They set the surprise down on his lectern, and when he opened the parcel his face turned red with emotion. As long as he lived, Louis Kissinger wouldn't forget that gesture. Four decades later, when he returned to his home town for the award of the Citizen's Gold Medal to his son, Louis Kissinger made sure that Gretlies Heyne, née Stäudtner, received an invitation to the ceremony, and she in turn will treasure that memory until the end of her days.

Heinz and Walter grew up in a typically bourgeois world.

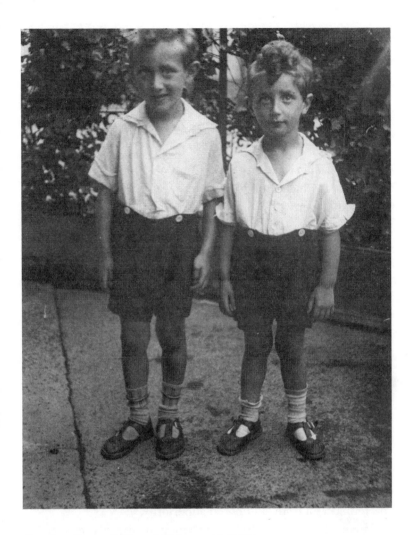

Carefree: Henry (left) and Walter, mid-1920s.

They both had piano lessons. Visits to the theatre were part of the compulsory programme from very early on. It wouldn't be fair to say that the sons liked going to the theatre. When receiving the city's medal of honour in that very same theatre, Henry recalled that he would rather have gone to a game at the local football club than a performance of *Fidelio*. But his father, a 'passionate music-lover' and opera fan, as Henry described him on that occasion, insisted on culture.

The family had a serving-girl who was practically part of the family and generally joined them at the dinner table. After the meal Louis checked the homework of his sons, who were incidentally considered bold at kindergarten and rascals at school. At first glance, the two boys look rather similar. Heinz is a head taller than Walter, but both have the narrow face and the curly, wavy, fair hair, the characteristic ears and above all, even then, those penetrating eyes.

On closer inspection, however, one can spot a difference that will become more and more pronounced over the years and decades: Walter looks like his mother, Heinz takes after his father. There is a photograph of Louis, probably from the 1930s, that could easily be his son when he was Secretary of State: the face of the teacher, who has by now been forced into retirement, has grown a little more round and shows the beginnings of a double chin, his eyebrows curve upwards towards the middle of his forehead, and his closed lips show a hint of a smile some-where between irony and bored superiority.

Much of this was already apparent in the features of his thirteen- or fourteen-year-old son. Heinz had a great deal of respect for his father, Louis enjoyed walking with him in the city park and often collected him from school. The fact that his father taught at a girls' school was unimportant. Boys of his age, he would later say, wouldn't have cast an eye at the opposite sex in those days. On those walks Heinz had his father all to himself. That was the exception. At home the disciplined, rather distant,

Chip off the old block: On the right, not Henry Kissinger, but his father Louis with David Kissinger, father of Louis and grandfather of Henry.

always industrious man mostly locked himself away in his study, and when he did so his sons weren't allowed near him.

Overall, Heinz was only an average pupil. He did take an active part in lessons, but, like his brother, he wasn't challenged enough at school and was inclined to practical jokes. His sense of humour was apparent even then. In English he managed a 'satisfactory'. But that changed. Apart from his unmistakable accent, the Harvard professor and American Secretary of State speaks impressive English. In his favourite subject, history, he got straight As in secondary school. History appealed to him even as a boy.

The two brothers read a lot, partly because there was no television in those days, and the Kissingers didn't have a radio, just a gramophone. Walter enjoyed the popular novels of Karl May, set in the remote Wild West of America. Heinz's friends saw him as a bookworm, and he was rarely spotted without a book under his arm. As he said in old age, he read Goethe, without at the time 'completely understanding him', and, 'with great enthusiasm', Schiller and also Dostoyevsky, but he was particularly fond of poems, historical novels, and history books.

The two boys got very good marks in religion. Small wonder, since their father saw their religious education both as a duty and as a matter close to his heart. After their third birthdays, he regularly took Heinz and Walter along to the synagogue. Jewish festivals and holidays were taken seriously, and the family kept kosher at home. The two brothers were also members of the Orthodox Jewish youth association, Esra, which met to sing, go on outings, and also to debate religious subjects.

However, the Kissingers' social life was not restricted to Jewish circles; quite the contrary, the family was fully and wholly integrated into the life of the city. Louis, for example, was a member of the Treu Fürth (True to Fürth) association, the aim of which was to resist attempts by Nuremberg to take over the city. And the boys had a large circle of friends, with whom they went on outings to the Alte Veste fortress or the suburb of Dambach, or to the Michaelmas Fair, where they rode on the Russian Wheel, a ferris wheel, on which Heinz usually felt sick.

And they went in for sports. Heinz and Walter were keen athletes, especially Walter, who even as a child took part in all the sporting events in Fürth, the more daring the better. When you see the eighty-year-old riding his horses or his motorbike, you can tell that little has changed. Heinz, too, discovered his passion for football when he was very young. His favourite positions were in goal and midfield. His school report for gymnastics reads only 'satisfactory', but his classmates remember Heinz 'playing football with every tin can even when he was little ... in the middle of Pfisterstrasse and in Theaterstrasse'.

Heinz, according to his former classmates, was not physically very strong, but 'quite fast'. In Fürth he played first of all in the Jewish sports club, then in the schoolboys' team of the Fürth club, of which he remained a loyal fan. Even if there is, as he says, no 'rational reason', Henry Kissinger continues to follow the results of the German leagues well into his old age, always in the hope that his club will make it into the first division.

For many years the German ambassador in Washington kept him up to date with the results; later it was a *Spiegel* editor who did so. Berndt von Staden, the ambassador in question, clearly remembers Secretary of State Henry Kissinger appearing in front of 300 correspondents in Washington's National Press Club: 'Suddenly he sees me and calls across the room: "There's the German ambassador. I thought we were on good terms, but clearly they aren't all that great, because I don't get the German football results any more." I wasn't terribly comfortable with that, because obviously everyone looked. Later, when I complained to my press attaché, who was responsible for these things, he said, "Didn't you know that the league doesn't play in January?"'

*

Paula and Louis had a series of friends whom they saw regularly. Life at 5 Marienstrasse was generally very sociable. When the adults came together in the Havdalah-Kränzchen (Havdalah Garland), plays were put on – nothing 'of any great literary importance', as Henry remembered in his old age, but good enough for pure entertainment. When the Kränzchenleut (Garland Folk), as they called themselves, corresponded outside of their theatrical meetings, they often did so in the form of self-penned poems. Unsurprisingly, the connection was maintained even when one or other of them left the city; they were always pleased to come back to the Kränzchen.

The Kissingers' circle of close friends still included Paula's childhood friends from Leutershausen. Babby and Karl Hezner had long been among Louis's closest friends as well. During the summer they saw each other often, because the family always spent the holidays at Paula's father's farm in Leutershausen. Heinz and Walter loved that, especially when their parents were travelling. Louis and Paula Kissinger travelled fairly regularly to Marienbad, and sometimes to Switzerland, but never, according to Henry, 'across the Main', meaning to northern Germany or the sea.

Then the two boys were allowed to stay with their grandparents, and naturally the grandchildren were spoiled to pieces by their grandfather and his wife, Fanny. Later, Henry and Walter would be the same with their own grandchildren. Every so often, they visited their paternal grandparents in Ermershausen; for David Kissinger's seventieth birthday they even wore smart sailor suits. They had little contact with the village children because they didn't visit very often. But they were always willing to join in a game of football.

Heinz and Walter spent their summer holidays in Leutershausen because they had good friends there. In the Hezners' two daughters, Erika and Lore, they found playmates who were ready for any adventure, and their grandfather's big garden was

All dressed up: Henry Kissinger and his brother Walter (front row, second and third from left) in sailor suits at the 70th birthday of their grandfather David Kissinger in Ermershausen. Also in the picture in the second row, second from left: Paula Kissinger. Next to her on the right: Louis Kissinger and beside him his father David Kissinger, the birthday boy. Back row, third from the back: Falk Stern from Leutershausen, Paula Kissinger's father.

ideal for games and experiments. And there were all kinds of animals in it. What child wouldn't love to go running after a chicken or try to catch a cat? And Leutershausen had one other special attraction: the Flussbad, the river swimming pool in the Altmühl.

So the summers in Leutershausen were the highlight of the year for the brothers. It was already an event when their grandfather collected them from the station with his coach and horses. It became particularly exciting when Heinz and Walter were allowed to ride on their new balloon-tyred bicycles from Leutershausen to Fürth. There's a photograph that may well capture their farewell: in the middle their dainty little mother, with her arms around her sons, looking at Heinz on her left, Walter on her right with his arm around his mother's hip, the boys in open-necked shirts, short trousers and knee-length woollen socks, their bicycles decorated with fresh flowers – the sort of summer idyll that people were familiar with in the bourgeois world of those years.

Heinz and Walter Kissinger were leading the uncomplicated life of two little boys enjoying a protected childhood in a sound, respected family, and with a large circle of friends. When it all came to an end overnight, when all their parents' close and distant acquaintances gradually turned away from them, apart from the Hezners, when Heinz and Walter were isolated and could no longer go to the Leutershausen lido, their world collapsed. 'The worst thing', Henry said in retrospect, 'was being parted from our German friends.' This caesura in the Kissinger family's life had a name: Hitler.

On 30 January 1933, Adolf Hitler was appointed Reich Chancellor by President Paul von Hindenberg. This was part of a legal process as set out in the constitution of the German Reich. And Hitler's appointment was also quite natural, because he

Sunday outing: Louis and Paula Kissinger with their children Henry (left) and Walter, mid-1930s.

was the head of what was now by some way the strongest party in the Reichstag – this despite the fact that for a long time the National Socialist German Workers' Party (NSDAP) had not played a particularly conspicuous part in the country's politics, had not been involved in a single election before 1924, and had even been banned for a time, having to operate under a different name.

In the 1920s, the relatively stable phase of the Weimar Republic, the party had bobbed about with a few percentage points, until its breakthrough came in the middle of September 1930: with 18 per cent of votes and 107 seats, it became the second-strongest party in the German parliament, after the Social Democrats (SPD). And the NSDAP was still a long way from the zenith of its meteoric rise. In late July 1932 the National Socialists took a good 37 per cent of the vote, won 230 seats in the Reichstag, and left all the other parties, including the SPD, far behind.

How can we explain this phenomenal success? First of all, through circumstances. The global economic crisis that struck Europe, Germany included, after the collapse of the New York stock exchange, had devastating consequences. In 1932 German national income was about 40 per cent below its 1929 level, and by the beginning of 1933 unemployment had reached unbelievably high levels: more than six million people in Germany were without work. The NSDAP's time had come. It had an answer for everything, because it had a programme, and it had a Führer to put it into effect.

Who was he? Who was the man who would finally decide the fate of whole peoples, who would ensure that millions of people were expelled and annihilated, and whose politics were also responsible for Heinz and Walter Kissinger's lives taking a new turn? Because we may assume it's unlikely that either of them would have had a great career in America without Hitler. Whether Heinz, as he later coquettishly remarked, would have spent his life as a teacher in Nuremberg, or whether, as someone suggested at a dinner with Helmut Kohl, he might even have become a teacher in Munich, remains an open question.

Adolf Hitler's career as party leader, Reich Chancellor, president and commander-in-chief of the Wehrmacht was not predetermined: far from it, the early biography of the man born in April 1889 in the Austrian town of Braunau am Inn shows all the signs of failure. He didn't finish secondary school, he was repeatedly rejected by the Academy of Art in Vienna, and from 1908 his home was in the city's men's hostels and refuges for the homeless. In the Great War he was promoted to corporal and awarded the Iron Cross, and was finally wounded in a poison-gas attack a few weeks before the armistice was signed.

After his convalescence, Hitler tried his hand at politics, joining the German Workers' Party, which after February 1920 repositioned itself ideologically and renamed itself the National-sozialistische Deutsche Arbeiterpartei (NSDAP). As Führer of the party after the end of July 1921, Hitler was one of the initiators of the failed Munich putsch of 8 and 9 November 1923. His detention in prison in Landsberg am Lech did not last long. At the end of February 1925, two months after his release, the NSDAP was re-established and, after a period of stagnation, finally took power in Germany.

In fact, when Hitler assumed power in Germany in his mid-forties, the party had already passed the peak of its popularity. The first signs of economic improvement were on the horizon, and in the November 1932 elections the Nazis lost some 4 per cent of their votes and more than thirty seats in the Reichstag. But an influential group around the scheming former Chancellor Franz von Papen believed they could harness Hitler and the NSDAP for their own purposes, and helped them to power. Once his party was in government, Hitler used all available methods to ensure that it remained there and consolidated its power.

That he succeeded in doing this is down to his actual and

perceived successes: he appeared to be whipping the country into shape, both at home and abroad. At least, that was how it looked to most observers, in Germany above all, but not only there. Large numbers of people helped him both at home and abroad. Many thought him personally responsible for the successes of economic and social policies, particularly the reduction of unemployment. Others were sympathetic to the thrust of his foreign policy. Most people underestimated him. And many, the German Jews among them, believed or hoped that things wouldn't be all that bad.

The fact that he was underestimated is down to the monstrosity of his plans, in which many people refused to believe even when they were being realized. But it was also because Hitler had stayed in the shadows during the assumption of power and had been barely visible. Behind the scenes, however, the new Reich Chancellor had no doubt about the direction of things.

In fact, the German Jews could have known what they were facing, since nothing had changed in the Nazis' twenty-five-point programme which had been available for anyone to read since 1922. According to this, 'Only those who are our fellow countrymen can become citizens. Only those who have German blood, regardless of creed, can be our countrymen. Hence no Jew can be a countryman.' There was no room there for misunderstanding.

As soon as the National Socialists were in power, on 1 April 1933 a Reich-wide boycott of Jewish businesses was set in motion. The action was suspended after a few days because the public showed surprising reservations, and some foreign governments intervened. The new rulers hadn't yet consolidated their position, not at home and certainly not abroad.

So at first they drew back from spectacular actions, and transferred their attention to administrative measures. With the

Law for the Restoration of the Professional Civil Service, passed on 7 April 1933, the persecution and oppression of the German Jews through administrative channels began – not least for Louis Kissinger. The measures taken over the coming weeks and months included, from the end of April 1933, the closure of public educational institutions to Jewish pupils and students, including Heinz and Walter Kissinger; and, from the end of July 1935, the exclusion of Jews from the Wehrmacht, as the Reichswehr had been called since declaring allegiance to its supreme commander, Adolf Hitler, 'Führer of the German Reich and People', in August 1934.

But discrimination against the Jews assumed a different quality with the Nuremberg Laws, announced at the Reich party convention of the NSDAP in mid-November 1935. The Reich party conventions were among the most important performances put on by the Nazis. After the first rallies of this kind, which Hitler had held between 1923 and 1929 in Munich, Weimar and Nuremberg, following the assumption of power the Franconian metropolis became the 'city of party conventions'. The Nazis cited historical grounds for this, among them the Imperial Diets of the Holy Roman Empire. And as far as the new rulers were concerned there was much to be said for this choice of location: the Nuremberg region had for years been one of the party's strongholds. The party conventions were tightly organized by Gauleiter Julius Streicher, who published, among other things, the anti-Semitic smear-sheet *Der Stürmer*.

So, every year from 1933 until 1938, at first for seven days and finally for eight, Nuremberg became the centre of the National Socialist movement. The preparations for the next, the seventh, party convention had been largely concluded when, in autumn 1939, war began with the German invasion of Poland, and the era of party conventions came to an end. Year after year until then, up to a million people, watching, marching, parading, or giving gymnastics displays, took part in the march pasts and inspections, all directed towards the Führer, Adolf Hitler. An impossibly grandiose backdrop was planned for the spectacle and built by his favourite architects, Albert Speer at their head. Occupying eleven square kilometres, the area was bigger than the Old Town of Nuremberg. Hitler's film director of choice, Leni Riefenstahl, captured, and aesthetically enhanced, the spectacle in two monumental documentary films.

Organizationally, the party conventions represented a huge logistical challenge. Hundreds of thousands of people, from every corner of the Reich, needed transport to the area around Nuremberg and food and lodging. Small wonder that the neighbouring towns also became involved in the running of the big event. And that included Fürth: in 1934, up to 70,000 visitors, most of them brought in on more than fifty special trains, arrived in the flag-bedecked city and were put up in two enormous campsites on the edge of Fürth. Numbers declined somewhat in the years that followed, but Hermann Göring, Prussian prime minister and commander-in-chief of the Luftwaffe, paid two visits to Fürth; and Hitler sometimes appeared in the city, if not during the Reich party conventions then, for example, to visit the theatre, as he did in February 1935.

Fürth's Jewish inhabitants tried to avoid their city as far as possible during those days. That included Heinz and Walter Kissinger, who generally stayed with their grandparents in Leutershausen. Only once did they experience the Nazis' big display, when they came home early by train to Nuremberg because the holidays were over. The situation, Walter recalled later in life, had something 'very ominous' about it, although as an eleven- or twelve-year-old he couldn't have said why he thought that.

Each Reich party convention was held under a different motto. The one in 1935 was celebrated as the Party Convention

Sucked into the spectacle: Hitler's Reichsparteitage (Reich Party Conventions) in neighbouring Nuremberg were also a major event for Fürth. This is the 'Party Day of Victory', summer 1933.

of Freedom. The Reichstag, in which only National Socialists now sat, was specially summoned to Nuremberg on 15 September to pass the so-called Nuremberg Laws. One of these, the Reich Citizen Law, deprived Jews of their rights as citizens, including the right to vote; the other, the Law for the Protection of German Blood and German Honour, forbade Jews, among other things, to have 'extramarital intercourse' with 'subjects of the German state or related blood', or to 'fly the Reich or national flag'.

In retrospect, it is astonishing that the German Jews should not have taken these laws as a signal and left the country in droves. But the opposite occurred: in 1935 even fewer Jews left Germany than had done so the previous year, just 21,000. Most of them still saw the country as their ancestral home. And who needlessly turns his back on his home for an unforeseeable future? There was also the fact that the journey was far from free. In order to emigrate, Jews had to leave the bulk of their possessions behind in Germany, and that greatly diminished their chances of being allowed in anywhere else.

Besides, many people read the Nuremberg Laws quite differently. Hannah Arendt, the Jewish philosopher who left in 1933 – first to Paris, then in 1941 to New York – later pointed out that the laws merely legalized a situation 'that had existed de facto for a long time'. Thus the Jews gained 'the impression that the Nuremberg Laws stabilized the new situation of the Jews in the German Reich'.

So most of them stayed, and watched their situation deteriorating month by month. Above all, their last possibilities for making a living were gradually being taken away from them. Passports belonging to Jews had been stamped with a red 'J' since October 1938; in June of that year, in Berlin alone 1500 Jews were arrested and deported to concentration camps; on 9 June the Munich synagogue, and on 10 August the main synagogue in Nuremberg, were torn down. A new kind of radicalization and brutalization was beginning to emerge.

And then it came, on the night of 9 November. The spark for Kristallnacht was a murder: on 7 November, Hershel Grynspan shot a German diplomat in Paris. Grynspan's parents, like 17,000 other Jews of Polish nationality, expelled from the German Reich at the end of October, had been forbidden entry to Poland, and had been wandering around in an undignified no-man's-land since then. For the National Socialists the Paris murder was the excuse they needed. Jewish shops were demolished and plundered, their flats stormed, their cemeteries defiled. More than ninety Jews lost their lives; 30,000 were arrested and placed in concentration camps.

Now, when it was too late, it finally became clear: the Jews no longer had any future in Germany. Of more than 550,000 who lived there when the National Socialists took power, just under a third, or about 180,000 had left the country. Among them, at the last minute, were the Kissingers: on 10 August 1938, the day the Nuremberg synagogue was destroyed, they reported to the police that they were leaving Fürth.

By doing so they had – Paula Kissinger most of all – drawn the conclusions from a situation that had been becoming untenable for years. On 6 April 1933, when Louis Kissinger signed the school reports for his class, he had no idea that they would be the last ones: the next day the Law for the Restoration of the Professional Civil Service came into force, taking away his right to work as a grammar-school teacher. On 2 May 1933, Louis Kissinger was forcibly dismissed. At the start of the 1933–4 school year he was, 'in accordance with the law passed by the Bavarian Ministry of the Interior on 9 October 1933', 'permanently retired'.

It was a blow from which the teacher would never fully recover. At first, no one dared to say whether things might take a turn for the better: hope, as we know, is the last thing to die.

And his pension was paid – until the end of his life, incidentally; after that the payments went to his widow. But that was small consolation. He was only forty-seven. And social exclusion follows hot on the heels of the loss of one's job. His former colleagues kept their distance from him – and not only those whose involvement in National Socialism went beyond party membership. Not a single person really stood by him.

No one knows how or whether Louis Kissinger would have got over this traumatic experience without his wife. He spoke of it even in old age; for example, on 14 August 1972, when celebrating his golden wedding in Switzerland with Paula and their sons and grandchildren. 'I will never forget', he said, turning to his wife and speaking in English, 'what she meant for me when I had to give up the job for which I had worked so hard and which had brought me such contentment. Her understanding gave me back my confidence in myself.'

At the time the situation also took its toll on Paula, because it wasn't just Louis's fellow teachers who kept their distance; their circle of friends and acquaintances rapidly diminished as well, and the Kissingers' lives became subject to greater and greater restrictions. And it wasn't only the parents who noticed, Heinz and Walter did too: they were no longer allowed to take part in most sporting events, and there was even a ban on attending their local club's home games at the Ronhof Stadium. Heinz, and sometimes Walter, occasionally went along anyway, ignoring the ban imposed by their concerned parents. They were worried. The boys, on the other hand, were not tormented by their parents' fears: 'All we risked', Heinz said later, 'was a smack.'

Even more serious than the prohibitions on sport and leisure were the sanctions affecting their schooling, at least as far as their parents were concerned. As Louis Kissinger could no longer teach at a city school, his sons weren't allowed to attend one either. In April 1933 the Nazis had limited the number of new admissions of Jews to public schools to 1.5 per cent. So Heinz and Walter attended the Jewish Realschule at 31 Blumenstrasse. Clearly they weren't sufficiently challenged there and soon got bored, which possibly explains the entries in the classbook describing Heinz as 'cheeky'.

One of the most oppressive aspects of the new situation was that the headquarters of the Fürth branch of the Hitler Youth was now in premises not far from the Kissingers' apartment. At first Heinz and Walter couldn't understand why they weren't allowed to join in as the uniformed boys passed by singing. That soon changed, though, because if they came too close to the marching boys they would be beaten up. Sometimes they were even intercepted outside their school, and when they first reached New York they would automatically cross the street when young men approached. The hope that friends they had known for years would stand up for them, or at least not round on them, was soon disappointed.

In fact, there were only two exceptions. There were two girls who didn't start regularly giving them a wide berth. Lore and Erika, the daughters of Karl and Babby Hezner, went on playing with the two boys when the Kissingers were in Leutershausen. But many things had changed for the worse in Paula's little home town. The inhabitants of Leutershausen, who had made Adolf Hitler an honorary citizen as early as July 1932, quickly adapted to the new times, and that meant, for example, that Heinz and Walter were no longer allowed to use the swimming pool in the river. Thinking back on the situation in Leutershausen in old age, Walter spoke of a 'microcosm' in which one could study how quickly a sound society could be poisoned by a regime.

So the children, who were less than ten and eleven when the Nazis came to power, were not immune from the increasing danger in which the family found itself. Increasingly often the parents had serious, concerned discussions with the Hezners. It was Karl Hezner who urged Louis Kissinger to leave the country early on. But Louis would have none of it, and even reacted with fury to his friend's advice: 'This is where we belong. We haven't done anything to anyone.'

For Louis Kissinger, Jewish faith and German citizenship had never been mutually exclusive; on the contrary, that was why he had joined the Central Association of German Citizens of Jewish Faith. He rejected the foundation of a special Jewish state in Palestine, as the Zionists demanded – unlike, for example, his brother Karl, his junior by eleven years, who was rather inclined towards the idea, having been locked up in a concentration camp for a year and a half. It was unambiguous support for integration that the association had, since its foundation before the turn of the century, seen as the best remedy for anti-Semitism. Its members were patriots including Louis Kissinger.

Like his father-in-law, Falk Stern, Louis's brother Karl had fought for the German cause in the First World War, and had been awarded the Iron Cross. And two first cousins of Louis Kissinger, who were in England when the war broke out, had had themselves ferried by coal-steamer to neutral Holland in order to join the German army as volunteers. Both were killed in the first year of the war.

Even in old age, Walter always wondered what his father would have done if the Nazis hadn't waged their campaign against the German Jews. Throughout his life, Louis Kissinger had been a committed patriot, so it is no surprise that he was still convinced, even in the mid-1930s, that Jews and Germans had a common future. He saw National Socialism as a fleeting phenomenon that the Germans would deal with sooner or later: 'They must recognize', he said time and again, 'that these people are below them.' It didn't occur to him that the Nazis were supported by a stable majority; he couldn't, or wouldn't, see that this broad support was the result of actual or imagined successes in the fields of the economy and politics, and later of warfare.

And Louis Kissinger was able to continue his work, albeit with restrictions. He was now teaching children who were forbidden to attend school regularly under Nazi rule. Of course, he knew that that would all come to an end abroad, because his language was German. He couldn't speak anything else, at least not a modern language, well enough to meet his own standards. If it had been up to him, the family would never have left the country, and that would have amounted to a death sentence.

It was Paula who finally made the decision. Her relationship with Germany was less sentimental than her husband's. It was based on realism. For her, the assumption of power by the Nazis and the radicalization of anti-Semitism were not unexpected. She had observed that Julius Streicher had been causing a furore since 1923 in the Nuremberg region with his smear-sheet *Der Stürmer*, and that there were few regions in which the Nazis had enjoyed such early successes as they had in Franconia, where Streicher had been Gauleiter since 1925. Consequently, the professional and social exclusion of the family that followed the Nazis' rise to power had not taken her completely by surprise.

So Paula Kissinger prepared to leave the country with her husband and children. First of all, she freshened up her school English, regularly met up with friends from the Jewish milieu to practise English conversation, and read only English-language books. It would be wrong to conclude from this that she couldn't get out of Germany quickly enough. She was attached to her homeland too. And she knew that emigration would only be possible by forfeiting large amounts of their fortune, however modest it might be. But above all, she was worried about her father. Falk Stern was ill with cancer, and emigration was unthinkable. Could he be left behind with no one to protect him?

Finanzamt Fürth (Bayern)
Bankkonto: Reichsbank Fürth (Bayern)
Bayer. Staatsbank Fürth (Bayern)
Postscheckkonto Nr. 1702 Nürnberg
Anlaufstunden: Montag mit Freitag von 8—12 Uhr
Fernruf Nr. 72421

Fürth (Bayern), 6. Mai 1938

An

...ie Geh. Staatspolizei Staatspolizei-
stelle Nbg.-Fürth in
FÜRTH/Bay.

Nürnbergerstr. 18

Gegenstand: Auswanderung; hier

steuerliche Prüfung.

(Zum Schreiben v. 27.4.38 Nr.
1312/VI).
Beilagen:

./.

Gegen die Auswanderung des
Handelsoberlehrers a.D. Louis
KISSINGER, geb. 2.2.1887, seiner Ehe-
frau Paula, geborene STERN, geb.
25.2.1901 und deren Kinder Alfred
Heinz geb. 27.5.1923 u. Walter Bernhard, geb. 21.6.1934, sämtl. wohnend
in FÜRTH/Bay., Marienstr. 5/II, be-
stehen vom steuerlichen Standpunkte
aus keine Bedenken.

Jn Vertretung:
gez. DITTMAR.

Beglaubigt
Steueresekretär.

*No remaining doubts: with its letter of 6 May 1938 to the Gestapo,
Fürth tax office grants permission for Louis Kissinger and his family
to leave the country.*

Paula Kissinger faced a difficult decision, probably the most difficult decision of her life. As things stood, though, she would have to say goodbye temporarily, either to her father or to her sons. After the Nuremberg Laws of September 1935 had imposed further restrictions on the Jews in Germany, she wrote to a cousin in the United States and asked if she could send her sons to her. The cousins had never seen each other, since even their mothers had never met; by the time Paula's mother was born, her elder sister had already emigrated to the USA.

Nonetheless, the family bond proved to be a tough one: Sarah Ascher was three years older than Paula Kissinger, was born in Brooklyn, and now lived in Larchmont on Long Island, in the immediate vicinity of New York City. She wanted to help Heinz and Walter, but because she didn't think she could assume responsibility for them, and probably also because she guessed how things were likely to develop in Germany, she encouraged Paula and Louis to emigrate to America with the children.

On 28 October 1937, Sarah Ascher signed an Affidavit of Support, thus providing the precondition for the Kissingers' immigration to the United States. The reason given in the affidavit for their emigration was the living conditions of Jews in Germany. The family, it says, spoke 'some English', but was not in a position to survive financially. She herself, the cousin stated, was a housewife; she earned US$80 per week, owned shares to the value of US$8000, had loans to a value of US$7000, and had savings totalling US$8000. This was enough to satisfy the US authorities that the four new arrivals would have sufficient support in their early days.

And so, on 24 April 1938, Louis Kissinger applied for passports because it was 'his intention to emigrate' with his family 'to the United States of America'. On 29 April the Gestapo issued the necessary documents, followed on 5 May by the police department in Nuremberg-Fürth, on 6 May by the Fürth tax office, and, also on 6 May, by the customs office. The

The documents that saved the day: on 11 May 1938 Fürth police headquarters issued passports for Louis, Paula, Henry and Walter Kissinger.

administrative charge of 12 Reichsmarks had been paid, and the passports arrived shortly afterwards. In August everything was prepared for the journey. It was time to say goodbye.

The most difficult part was the visit to Leutershausen, to the dying Falk Stern and his wife Fanny, Paula's stepmother. For the first time in their lives the sons saw their father cry. Having spent his whole life disciplined, detached, strict and composed at all times, Louis Kissinger was overwhelmed by the pain of separation and lost his composure. If anything was fixed in the children's memories for the rest of their lives, it was this moment and what it represented; seeing one's parents helpless, defenceless and humiliated was a traumatic experience.

For Heinz and Walter events since January 1933 had, of course, been a bad experience. But they were young, the future was theirs. They didn't suffer the pain that was being inflicted on their parents. Yet if there was something capable of unsettling the brothers even in old age, it was the memory of their parents' suffering. Typically, Walter's voice failed when he tried to talk about this in 2004 in front of a camera. And in 1975, when Henry was asked by journalists why he was accepting the medal of honour of the city of Fürth, he stated quite clearly that he was doing it for his parents' sake.

On 10 August 1938 Louis Kissinger officially notified police headquarters in Fürth that he and his family were leaving. Ten days later they were on the way to London, where they stayed with Berta and Sigmund Fleischmann, Paula's aunt and her husband who had run the butcher's shop in Fürth, and whose lodger Paula had been when she was going to school in Fürth. Just in time, the Fleischmanns had correctly interpreted the signs and emigrated to England, and they now ran a small bed and breakfast in Golders Green. The four Kissingers briefly

Farewell to Europe: the Kissingers and relatives from Fürth in Golders Green, London, 28 August 1938, two days before their crossing to America. Front: Walter (left) and Henry Kissinger. Back, left to right: Sigmund Fleischmann, Paula Kissinger, Berta Fleischmann and Louis Kissinger.

stopped off there before finally, on 30 August, sailing from Le Havre to New York on the *Île de France*.

Almost as soon as they arrived, news from Germany, particularly of Reichskristallnacht on 9 November 1938, began to reach Louis and Paula. The picture gradually fell into shape for the emigrants. First of all, Falk Stern had to sell the house on the Marktplatz in Leutershausen, which he had bought with his brother in 1904, and in which his daughter Paula and his grandsons Heinz and Walter had enjoyed happy times. The new owners did put up the sick man and his wife for some time, until the pogroms began in Leutershausen, as early as the middle of October 1938. On 18 October, Falk Stern moved to his sister Minna's house in Fürth. Paula's father died there on 26 May 1939.

Like her sister Berta, Minna was married to a butcher. Unlike Berta and her husband Sigmund, Minna and her husband, Max Fleischmann, stayed in Fürth because Minna didn't want to leave her dying brother behind. In 1942 Minna and Max Fleischmann were deported and murdered, Minna in Theresienstadt, Max in Auschwitz. Their sister-in-law, Falk Stern's second wife Fanny, Paula's stepmother, also did not survive the extermination of European Jewry.

Most members of the Kissinger family suffered a similar fate. Among those who did survive were David Kissinger and his three sons, Louis, Karl and Arno. Karl lived in Ingolstadt on the Danube, where he married the wealthy Paula Friedmann in 1923; the two of them went on to run her father's successful shop, the Friedmann Shoe House. As soon as the Nazis assumed power in the country, on 30 June 1933, he was arrested by a member of the city administration and deputy SS standardbearer, and on the same day 'at 4.30 in the afternoon' locked up in Dachau concentration camp as prisoner number 2339. In

August 1933 he was transferred to the Aussenlager, or sub-camp, and assigned to the street-mending unit.

There Karl Kissinger, as he wrote in April 1947 to a former fellow prisoner in Elland in Yorkshire, was subjected to various kinds of abuse. An SS man, identified by name, 'dragged him during their work into a nearby wood' where he beat him 'most cruelly'. The abuse reached a peak in the middle of October 1933 when another named SS Sturmbannführer, 'a monster, barbaric, sadistic', tried to 'extort confessions about supposed contacts with Russia' from the Jewish prisoners. When 'that failed, on 18.10.33 all Jews had to perform punishment drills and pull rollers over softened ground, an unimaginably cruel procedure. When', Karl Kissinger wrote, looking back in 1947, 'late in the afternoon I told him on behalf of my utterly exhausted comrades: you can have us all shot, but we are not going to admit to something that we haven't done, he brutally replied, "Without a confession none of you will leave the camp alive."'

The fact that Karl Kissinger, like many of his fellow prisoners, had fought for Germany in the First World War and been decorated no longer mattered. Still, his wife, who had good connections in Ingolstadt, managed to have him freed in December 1934, after eighteen months. He had, however, to agree to the sale of the shop. After that, he moved to Munich with his wife and their three children, Herbert, Erwin and Margot, Heinz and Walter's cousins. In 1937 the family managed to emigrate to Palestine.

Like most of the survivors in the Kissinger family, Karl set foot on German soil again after the end of Nazi rule. He lived in Munich for a while in the early 1950s, before he and his wife finally settled in Florida. After that, Karl Kissinger repeatedly returned to Germany, whether for business or for health-cures. And if it could be arranged, he would also pay a visit to Ermershausen, the place where he had spent his childhood and youth.

Karl's brother Arno, Heinz and Walter Kissinger's other uncle on their father's side, was also a businessman. As a representative of a company selling optical lenses, he travelled much of the world, including the United States of America, and his two nephews from Fürth profited by this, since their uncle often came back from his travels with a present. In the mid-1930s Arno Kissinger recognized that the Jews had no future in Germany, settled in Stockholm as a representative of the American Optical Company, and in 1943 married Erika Mayer, also from Germany. After the pogroms of Reichskristallnacht had left no doubt about the fate that faced the Jews in Germany, early in 1939 Arno Kissinger also persuaded his father to move to Sweden. Until his death, David Kissinger lived with his son and daughter-in-law in Stockholm.

Perhaps because he lived in neutral Sweden, and also because he was the only brother to have stayed in Europe, Arno Kissinger was the one with whom the sisters who had stayed behind in Germany retained contact, while that was possible. In the end, they all – Selma, Ida and Fanny, and almost all of their family members – lost their lives. The ones who managed to get out in time, including Louis and Paula Kissinger, tried to get their relatives to join them, but in vain. In some cases the papers were already on the way, but it was too late.

Almost all of them, like the members of the Stern family, were initially deported to Izbica. This little town not far from Lublin, had been annexed by the Generalgouvernment which was set up after the German invasion of Poland in mid-October 1939. Here, in the heart of Poland, the German occupiers built four of the six extermination camps in which the Jews of Europe were systematically and industrially murdered from the summer of 1941 onwards. Izbica was a transit station for transports from various cities and regions of Germany and Austria, as well as from the Theresienstadt ghetto, which served, among other things, as a transit camp for the Jews of central and western

Europe. From Izbica the victims were taken to the gas chambers of Sobibor and Belzec.

Those deported to Izbica included almost all the members of the Stern and Kissinger families still living in the Fürth region. Most of them will have been on the transport assembled between 22 and 24 March 1942 in the region of Fürth and Nuremberg, which included 237 Jews from Fürth.

Years later, in mid-May 1953, Arno Kissinger wrote to his brother Karl recounting what he knew about the fate of their sister Selma Blättner. On 22 May 1942 she and her husband, Max Blättner, contacted Arno Kissinger from Frankfurt for the first time and told him that they were about to go travelling but that they couldn't give him an address. Presumably they were assigned to the transport that left Frankfurt on 11 June 1942. On 7 July, Selma Blättner sent a postcard with her new address: Izbica, Block 3, 445a. It was the only message that reached her brother from the camp. Neither the packages nor the money that he sent to them, the latter through a bank, reached their destination.

Louise Blättner, Max and Selma's daughter, sent one last letter, dated 19 January 1943, to her uncle in Stockholm. Six weeks later she was, to his knowledge, seen once more in Berlin. After that, Arno Kissinger wrote to his brother Karl in 1953, she too was deported. The same fate was suffered by Fanny and Ida, Karl, Louis and Arno's other sisters. Fanny Rau, her husband Jakob, and her son Norbert were also deported to Izbica and then killed, as were Ida Friedmann and her husband Siegbert.

Nevertheless, Ida and Siegbert had managed to send their three children, Bella, Julius and Lisa, to London. They themselves did not get the life-saving visas that had enabled Louis and Paula Kissinger to emigrate to America. In one of their last messages to their children in London they wrote: 'We are glad to know you are well; we too are, thank heavens, healthy and in good spirits ... Stay healthy and write to us often. Loving greetings and kisses from your mother.' Shortly afterwards Ida and Siegbert Friedmann were deported from Mainstockheim to Izbica. One can easily imagine the fate that would have awaited Louis, Paula, Heinz and Walter Kissinger if they had not managed to leave Germany.

They survived, though, far from Germany and Europe, in an unfamiliar world. The country in which the family of four arrived for the first time in 1938 was not in a happy state. The global economic and political fault lines that had played a part in Hitler's meteoric rise had their origins here in the United States. From the end of October 1929 until the beginning of July 1932 the American stock market had gone into unstoppable decline, dragging with it everything that depended upon it, directly or indirectly; 85,000 businesses went bankrupt, and one in four Americans who wanted to work were unable to find a job. When the Kissingers came ashore in New York, the site of the stock market crash, America was still caught up in the crisis.

But there was hope, connected with the name of Franklin D. Roosevelt. The thirty-second president of the United States had entered the White House early in May. On the way there, the Democratic candidate had committed himself and his fellow countrymen to a new start, the New Deal. No one, not even the president, could say exactly what it would be like, what lay behind it. There was no fully formulated strategy, but there were two large bundles of legal and administrative measures to be got off the ground in 1933 and 1935. Nothing of the kind had ever been attempted before in American history.

At least as crucial as these measures themselves, which were to prove only partially successful, was the will to change. And that was what the president himself, only fifty when he entered office, represented. Having contracted polio as an adult, since when he had been confined to a wheelchair, Franklin D.

Roosevelt stood for the conviction that any situation could be mastered with confidence, courage and an iron will. With these same qualities he would, in the late 1930s, face Hitler and finally force the German dictator to his knees. With them he would, from the moment he entered office, master the severe crisis that still had America in its grip.

From that point of view, F.D.R., as he was already known at the time, embodied the virtue that would provide opportunities and would offer the starting point for the sorts of lives that Heinz and Walter Kissinger would forge for themselves. That could not yet have been foreseen, however, because when the two boys arrived in their new homeland, America faced another winter with up to nine million unemployed. New arrivals were not especially welcome, even if they had had to turn their backs on their homeland because they had no future there.

For as long as they lived, Louis and Paula Kissinger would not forget what that new start had meant for them and their children, how confidence and resignation were always in the balance. They were lucky; they found and used the opportunities that the country was able to offer. They became Americans, and were proud of it. Thirty years after their arrival, having been invited by their now-famous son to witness the inauguration of President Nixon for his second term of office, Paula Kissinger was overwhelmed by that feeling. Now in her seventies, she wrote to her brother-in-law Arno Kissinger in Stockholm to say that it filled her with pride 'to be part of this country which, in spite of its internal divisions and many unsolved problems, is still a great country in which to live and which still provides unlimited opportunities for the many who seek them'.

That was one side, but there was another. Louis in particular never forgot how bleak their beginnings had been. Even decades later, when he celebrated his golden wedding in Switzerland with his wife, children, grandchildren and brother Arno, he remembered the 'hopelessness' that he and Paula had felt when they had set about building a 'new future' in this 'new country'. 'You can imagine', he wrote to his family in Germany at the end of 1979, 'that we had to endure difficult, anxious years before we could find our feet.'

When Louis, Paula, Heinz and Walter Kissinger stepped ashore in New York in 1938, they found themselves in a very alien world. The culture shock was considerable. The four of them had barely ever left the confines of their Franconian home. Certainly, Paula had spent a few months working as an au pair in north Germany; and she and her husband had travelled more or less regularly to Marienbad, and sometimes to Switzerland. But this was something else. This was New York, and New York was a city with over a million inhabitants, with skyscrapers, incredibly dense traffic, a deafening noise level, a boundless selection of shops, restaurants and bars, and, above all, a huge number of people. All of these things combine to make the individual seem even tinier than he is already.

When the exiles arrived, what sort of state were they in? They had an inadequate mastery of the language, modest financial means, and, not least, a bad conscience. Precisely because they had got out, because they had had to leave others behind, because there was nothing more they could do for them, because in many cases they wouldn't even learn what had become of them, they felt guilty and miserable. Besides, they didn't even have a roof over their heads. Almost all new arrivals initially fetched up in the city's hostels, with their big dormitories divided between men and women, before moving to the first modest lodgings of their own.

That came as a shock to many of the older people, since it was only then that they realized what emigration really meant. For the younger people it was generally easier. Plainly, however, this fate left its mark on them as well. That would include the relationship between the two brothers: we can't know how the bond between them would have developed without this disruption in their lives, but as it was, they were bound for life by that 'common fate' of which Henry would still speak in his old age. 'We were always in contact, even during the war,' Henry says, 'and even now we see each other regularly … I have the greatest respect for my brother, and I trust him completely. So we speak often and regularly about personal problems.'

Compared with other people, the two brothers found a blessing in disguise when fate drove them to America. They entered their new homeland at an age when abandoning one's old ways, losing social status, finding one's bearings in a new world, and switching to a foreign language, are not yet much of a problem. And they weren't just leaving beautiful memories behind, for the last few years in Germany had been terrible.

There was something adventurous about the journey, too. For most Europeans, America, and New York in particular, epitomized the big, wide world. Even late in his life Walter remembered entering the harbour of the metropolis at night – the light-drenched skyline and the Statue of Liberty. He had, rather intuitively, understood the great symbolic significance that this landmark had for the country, the city and its inhabitants, which now included the four immigrants from Fürth.

He and his brother didn't feel homesick, but the same couldn't be said of their parents. They had left their Franconian home with the feeling that they would not be seeing it again, at least not for the foreseeable future. For them, the journey and the early days in America were not an adventure but a difficult new beginning. They had no plan for their lives. How could they have had? Where was one to start? Where would they find a roof over their heads? Would it ever be possible to reach the old standard of living that they had enjoyed in Germany? They had had to leave almost everything behind.

That included their furniture and all their portable pos-sessions. Over the years they had assembled quite a collection. Because in January 1927 senior master Louis Kissinger had produced a Fahrnisverzeichnis, a list of furniture, for the records of the district teachers' association, we know that these were the typical furnishings of a bourgeois family in Germany at the time. As the family did not move house until they had to flee the country, little can have changed other than for items that the teacher had acquired for his two growing sons, such as a piano or the bicycles that are not yet listed in the 1927 Fahrnisverzeichnis.

Otherwise, everything is painstakingly recorded, from the four cupboards and tables, the seventeen chairs and five beds, bedclothes, clothes, shoes and linen, to a lady's and a man's watch, silver cutlery and cheese-knives to the value of 30 Reichsmarks. Altogether, the value of the Kissinger family's movable possessions in 1927 came to just under 23,000 Reichs-marks, including 'music and books'. Apart from a few suitcases with clothes and their most important papers, everything was left behind in Fürth when the Kissingers left the city. Admittedly, the furniture was to be sent on afterwards. But given the arbitrary power of the rulers in Germany, it would have been sensible not to bet on it.

The family were lucky in their misfortune, though, because an uncle in Pittsburgh, who died in 1933, had left a modest inheritance. Louis Baehr had been a guest at the wedding of Louis and Paula Kissinger, and later had visited them and their sons in Fürth. As his wife's family owned a department store in Pittsburgh, Louis Baehr didn't need to worry about his live-lihood, and his nephews in Fürth occasionally benefited too: on special occasions, Henry and Walter's uncle would sometimes give them small gifts of money.

So, the inheritance was enough to keep the new arrivals' heads above water for the first months in New York, and, most importantly, it allowed them to move into an apartment of their own. But instead of the five-room flat in the picturesque Old Town of Fürth, they now found themselves in a two-room apartment in the rather run-down Bronx, and the idea of a serving-girl, a comfort that would have been taken for granted back home, was now quite unthinkable.

Work, too, was hard for Louis Kissinger, who did everything he could to find a teaching post. But in New York in the late 1930s that was quite hopeless, because of the economic misery of the Depression, and also because of the language barrier. Overall, where the new language was concerned, the family was in quite a good state. Not only had Heinz and Walter learned English at the Realschule in Fürth, but a month after their arrival they found places at George Washington High School, an excellent institution at the time, so from the very beginning they had a head start in the new language. And their parents insisted that English was spoken at home.

Heinz and Walter quickly mastered their new language, although in different ways. Heinz was the only one who changed his name. The other three kept theirs, although the pronunciation was Americanized. Louis remained Louis, Paula remained Paula, Walter remained Walter, but Heinz was now Henry. At the same time, he was the brother who never lost his German accent, and perhaps never wanted to lose it. Henry was only a year older than Walter, and Walter was soon perfectly assimilated in the new language; but we must bear in mind that from late 1944 Henry spent a few years in Germany, when he used his mother tongue again.

Unsurprisingly, their parents retained their characteristic accent until the end. They were quite old to be immersing themselves in a new language. But neither were they completely new to English; on the contrary, Paula had systematically prepared for their new life in this respect, and Louis, too, spoke better English than most immigrants. And they both took lessons to improve their knowledge.

However, to practise the teaching profession, in which linguistic mastery is paramount, this was not enough – at least not for Louis Kissinger, who set very high standards for himself in this regard as in all others. So, in the mind of a man who could speak fluent Latin and ancient Greek, an additional hurdle was erected. With a classical scholar's scruple, the fear of linguistic blunders became a handicap and further reduced his already minimal chances of returning to his beloved teaching profession.

So, one thing led to another. Insecure in English, increasingly often Louis Kissinger preferred to stay silent, which discouraged social contacts. It was a terrible burden for him not to be able to feed his family. Furthermore, the bad news from Germany kept coming in. After the November pogroms, of which they had learned shortly after their arrival in America, Louis knew that some of his family had reached safety literally at the last minute, and he also knew that there was nothing he could do for the ones who had been left behind. The feeling of impotence was oppressive.

Louis suffered and became depressed. Life in the metropolis didn't help. By now in his early fifties, he was the only one of the four new arrivals who adapted to his new environment only by very slow degrees. It is quite possible that this caused the pains in his stomach which became worse over time. Repeatedly he confessed to his wife: 'I am the loneliest person in this big city.'

Paula Kissinger knew that she had to do something. Fortunately, that was in her nature. She was considerably younger than Louis, and being still in her thirties she found adapting to her new conditions easier than he did. Her confidence and flexibility helped Paula not to see language as a crucial barrier. Admittedly her English wasn't perfect, and her German accent was impossible to ignore, but that didn't greatly bother her. She spoke unselfconsciously and didn't trouble herself about her mistakes. The main thing was that she could communicate.

So Paula started asking around in immigrant circles and trying to find a job. She was referred to the Council of Jewish Women, where it was suggested that she should go into catering. Luckily, Paula was free of prejudices and anxieties about status, and the fact that she actually hated cooking, after having run her father's household as a young woman, was neither here nor there. Now it was a matter of feeding and lodging the family.

So she took a course and learned how people cooked and mixed drinks in America. Now she even found she enjoyed cooking. She soon understood the business, and later the source of her livelihood also became her hobby. Paula Kissinger went on providing party services at a time when her son Henry was already making his way in Washington, always on condition that the customers made no use of her name. At first they kept to this rule, but then some of them couldn't resist the temptation and revealed the secret of the supplier with the famous name. It was only then that Paula gave up her catering service.

When she started the business it wasn't a luxury but a bitter necessity. Times were hard. The money that her business brought in wasn't nearly enough to see the family through hard times, and if they were to survive, the sons had to do their bit. A year after their arrival in New York they started working. Walter delivered newspapers early in the morning, before school, and Henry took a job in a shaving-brush factory. As he had to work during the day, he switched to evening school at George Washington High. However, the two boys' scholarly achievements didn't suffer; they were young, their father had got them into the proper frame of mind for school, and they knew that a good education was the key to a better future.

Soon they were able to concentrate fully on school again, for in 1940 their father found a job – not as a teacher, but in the accounts department of a metal processing company. It belonged to acquaintances from Franconia, who had made the leap before the Kissingers did. The job wasn't especially well paid, but at least Louis Kissinger was doing regular work. That did a great deal to help his self-esteem, and contributed to the family's income.

Paula's business was going increasingly well, too. She liked her new job, and she enjoyed cooking because it got a terrific response. She was an excellent cook, and although she herself only ever ate kosher, she also understood non-kosher cuisine. She was a cultivated and communicative woman, so news of her abilities and her services soon got round – among Jews, but also among non-Jews. Her customers came from every different walk of life, which in turn granted Paula an insight into the workings and rules of American society.

She made friends with some of her customers and immediately benefited from a cardinal American virtue: helpfulness. Some of her affluent customers were as moved by the family's fate as they were by Paula's commitment to her work, and they helped where they could. By now, though, the Kissingers hardly had to rely on such assistance. The parents' income was sufficient to support them, and enough for a new apartment. Two years after their arrival in the city they moved with their sons to Washington Heights.

The narrow northern tip of Manhattan – opposite the Bronx, separated from it by the Harlem River, and at the topmost point of the island – owes its name to a military fort in which George Washington and his entourage were sometimes quartered during the American War of Independence. Hence, too, the name of the main arterial road to the west, Fort Washington Avenue. Here, at number 615, not far from Fort Tryon Park, the Kissingers moved into an apartment. The parents stayed there until the end of their lives.

The apartment was very spacious for the times, like many of those in the area. The original inhabitants had had to give it up after the global economic crisis, and the new arrivals sought and found ways of giving themselves a faint sense of security in this strange new world; if they didn't have enough money for the flat, part of it would be rented out. Since the early 1930s Washington Heights had been increasingly attracting Jewish inhabitants. By the end of the decade the district had become a centre for Jews from Germany, who ironically called their new home the 'Fourth Reich'.

That was not entirely advantageous for the new arrivals. It was certainly reassuring to know that one wasn't alone, that other people here shared the same fate, and that one could communicate with them because they spoke the same language. Soon there were shops and restaurants that could hardly have been more German. On the other hand, this milieu not only hampered acclimatization, it also encouraged a certain tendency to ghettoization, and that in turn reinforced latent resentments. Anti-Semitic attacks, which were not uncommon in America at this time, were increasing. They frightened many people who had only escaped such things with great difficulty, particularly those who had come from Germany and who, once the war broke out, were seen as 'enemy aliens' or a 'fifth column' because of their origins.

The Kissingers were largely spared this dark side of things. When they came here from the Bronx they were already quite acclimatized, so they didn't risk being drawn back into the German milieu. And Sarah Ascher lived there, the cousin who had helped Paula and her family to leave Germany, and whom Paula first met after their arrival in New York. They were now friends as well as relations, and of course it helped the new arrivals that Sarah had been born in Brooklyn, which meant she had known the city and the country since she was a child.

Now it was most convenient that their furniture had arrived from Germany. Of course, Louis and Paula didn't just have material values in mind. They wanted to offer their sons a standard of living comparable to the one they had enjoyed in their old homeland, but also to give them an appropriate social and cultural environment. School provided a good basis, but the parents wanted more. So Paula often invited guests, particularly younger people, in order to give Henry and Walter a chance of expanding their horizons by exchanging ideas with other people. And when the financial situation allowed, the music-loving parents also revived another Fürth tradition and went to concerts with their sons.

Neither would religious instruction be ignored here in the New World. The family belonged to the Orthodox K'hal Adath Yeshurun community, which was founded by immigrants. Busy as she was with her work, Paula hardly found time to take an active part in the life of the community. Louis, however, regularly took his sons to the synagogue. For the time being, they followed their father. They knew how much his faith meant to him, and what a comfort it was in these hard times. Later, to their father's sorrow, there was a parting of the ways, as Henry and Walter became estranged from Jewish Orthodoxy.

One of the bright spots in their father's life was his sons' success. For all the grief at what they had had to leave behind, for all the concern for those they had been unable to help, it was lucky that at least their own children could live in a free country and work towards their future. And they did so with great success. They were the pride of their parents. Henry was now studying at City College in New York and considering going into accountancy, following the path that his father had taken in America. Walter initially worked in a garage, because motor cars had long been a passion of his. But history, in the form of the very man who had driven them from Germany, was soon to catch up with them.

*

When the Kissingers left Europe in the summer of 1938, Europe was on the brink of war, and Germany was the driving force behind it. Hitler had introduced compulsory military service in March 1935. A year later German troops had invaded the demilitarized zones of the Rhineland, and in March 1938 Austria was annexed to the German Reich – all signs of the coming storm. Hitler was given an easy ride because the other world leaders either kept their heads down or even cooperated with him: Great Britain, France and fascist Italy looked on as in March 1939, Germany invaded Czechoslovakia. And while London and Paris responded to the German attack on Poland on 1 September 1939 with a declaration of war, they did not immediately begin hostilities against the aggressor.

The Soviet dictator Josef Stalin even signed a pact with the German dictator, so that he could take part in the campaign of plunder in eastern central Europe. They would all pay a high price sooner or later. In Spring 1940, following the German invasions of Denmark, Norway, and Belgium, the Netherlands and Luxembourg, France was militarily defeated within a few weeks. Great Britain stood on the abyss for a year, and an unparalleled campaign of extermination rolled across the Soviet Union after the German invasion of 22 June 1941.

So how did America, the Kissingers' new homeland, respond to all this? It was reserved and strictly neutral – at least Congress was, and the wider public. Since August 1935 a raft of laws had forbidden any direct or indirect political or military intervention. It was the president, Franklin D. Roosevelt, who tried to steer things gradually in the direction of intervention. Political measures such as the recall of the American ambassador from Berlin, with which Roosevelt reacted to the pogroms of 10 November 1938, were increasingly flanked by military measures, especially after the defeat of France. The president was preparing his country to enter the war.

This was an enormous challenge, not least because the United States was far from ready for war. And apart from the European theatre, there was a second arena that increasingly impinged upon America's interests. After Japan had invaded Manchuria in September 1931 and, now allied with Germany, declared war on China in July 1937, in this area too, the president was wondering about the correct reaction.

The aggressors gave him his answer in both cases: on 7 December 1941 the Japanese attacked the American Pacific fleet at its base in Pearl Harbor in Hawaii, and four days later the German Reich declared war on the USA. Now the question was no longer whether, but when and where American troops would be deployed. The country found itself overnight in the biggest military confrontation of its history, because when the USA entered the war, the European and Asian wars were joined together in a global, Second World War.

Immediately after the outbreak of war, all men between the ages of twenty and forty-four were registered for military service. Millions volunteered. Overall, by the end of the war more than sixteen million Americans had joined the war effort. Among them were Henry and Walter Kissinger. One fought the Japanese in the Pacific, the other the Germans in Europe. For the first time since the family's escape, one of the four returned to Germany – as a soldier.

The story of Heinz and Walter

Part Two: The Homecoming

It's a special day. How many times has Henry Kissinger come to Germany over the past few decades! And was not each visit a homecoming? But today, 8 May 2005, is rather different. Today is the sixtieth anniversary of the German Reich's unconditional capitulation. That was the day the Second World War came to an end, in Europe at least. The prime minister of Hessen, Roland Koch, asked Henry to talk about his memories of that time. There was a good reason for the request, because it was at that time that Henry returned to the land of his childhood and early youth, where he 'spent fifteen months with the army of occupation on Bergstrasse and lived in Heppenheim'.

Nevertheless, his acceptance of the invitation could not be taken for granted, because, as he tells his listeners, Henry does not 'normally speak about personal experiences'. But that day, 'when the guns fell silent', changed his life for good; that first stay in Germany since his family's expulsion marked a 'turning point' in Henry Kissinger's life. And the old man talking to the Germans in Darmstadt today explains why that was.

Characteristically, he does so in the third person and in the plural. In that respect, Henry remains true to his principles and avoids being personal. Instead, he talks about the 'generation of those who emigrated from Germany in the 1930s' and who, 'independent of their own experiences during the Nazi period, retained a special relationship with the land of their birth'. 'They remembered those Germans who had stuck by them in spite of the dictatorship.' The audience sense that he had had that experience; and Henry knows that he is talking about the Hezners.

He states in Darmstadt that after the end of his official period of service he 'volunteered to stay another year'. That's not something somebody does if he has burnt all his bridges, if he is indifferent to the country and the people who expelled him and his family, or, indeed, if he hates them. Certainly, Henry never considered returning to his old homeland for good. He was too grateful, seven or eight years after emigration, to his new homeland. He was too fond of the 'carefree way' in which America took him and his family in. He valued too highly the 'better life' that he had been offered on the other side of the Atlantic after his escape from Germany.

But since setting foot on German soil again for the first time after his escape, he has been filled with a mission, a task: the maintenance of relationships between his new homeland and his old one. That as security adviser and Secretary of State he wasn't always over-scrupulous in his treatment of German governments, notably that of Willy Brandt, is neither here nor there. Now, after the end of the Cold War, and the end of the conflict between East and West, the important thing, more than ever, is good transatlantic relations.

In particular, the generation of emigrants, Henry explains to his audience in Darmstadt, grows 'uneasy when America is attacked as being imperialist or semi-authoritarian or with other terms from the lexicon of anti-American rhetoric'. These days of growing criticism of American politics and the war in Iraq are not good times for thin-skinned people. And Henry Kissinger, the American with German roots, is one of those.

Henry came to Europe in early November 1944. He was the first member of the Kissinger family to set foot on European soil after their expulsion. He came as a soldier. In February 1943 he had been called up to the United States forces. Like his maternal grandfather thirty years previously, he was doing his duty. But unlike Falk Stern, who fought in the German army in the First World War, and who might have come into contact with American forces when he was deployed on the western front, from the summer of 1944 his grandson fought in the American army against the German Wehrmacht.

Until this happened, until the USA and her allies launched the biggest invasion in history in Normandy in June 1944, Henry Kissinger had been part of a group of young Americans who were allowed to undertake a special army training programme after call-up. Henry was lucky, as he was so often later in his life. He hadn't been exactly delighted to be called up, he would rather have gone on studying at City College. But he was to be able to do just that, albeit in a different place, with the help of the army. For just over a year, he studied at Lafayette College in Easton, Pennsylvania, which gave him the opportunity to take twelve classes, including scientific disciplines, and also, from time to time, the chance to go to New York and spend the weekend with his parents.

In April 1944, however, it was all over. Henry Kissinger was assigned to G Company of the 335th Infantry Regiment, preparing for the landing in Europe along with the 84th Infantry Division in Louisiana. It was there that he met Fritz Gustav Anton Kraemer, who had left Germany as an opponent of Hitler, and who became Henry Kissinger's mentor and sponsor, the man who discovered his talents. In September the 20,000-strong division received its marching orders, and shortly afterwards they embarked in New York for France. On 9 November 1944 the division, near Aachen and under heavy fire, crossed the border into Germany. The unit took part in the resistance to the German Ardennes offensive, then advanced to Hanover and, among other things, freed Ahlem concentration camp.

So the American soldier Henry was back in the country that the German schoolboy Heinz had left six years previously. There he acted at first as interpreter and driver to the commanding general, was then made part of the counter-intelligence section of the division, and finally was detailed to counter-espionage.

The discoverer: Henry Kissinger during the Second World War with his mentor and patron Fritz Kraemer.

Sixty years later, he recalled: 'The chief commander of our division assumed that because of my German background and my knowledge of languages I'd be able to spot any German spy with the naked eye. Luckily, that supposed ability was never put to the test because my division never encountered a German spy, or at least never unmasked one.'

As soon as hostilities were over, Henry went in search of friends and relations. At the end of 1946 he even took the train to Stockholm, where his grandfather David Kissinger, now eighty-six, and one of his sons, Henry's uncle Arno, had survived the Nazi period. First, though, he was drawn to the region where he had spent his childhood and part of his youth. Henry visited Nuremberg, Fürth, and, last but not least, Leutershausen.

There he spent a lot of time looking for the Hezners, and was relieved to find them in good health. Sixty years later his brother Walter still thought it was a 'miracle that Karl Hezner survived the Nazi era'. The American occupying forces saw things quite differently. Probably because of a denunciation, Karl Hezner was suspected of being a 'secret Nazi'. Henry Kissinger soon put them right about that.

In that respect at least, the oldest son was able to put good news in his letters to his parents in America. But such things were the exceptions. Everything else he saw in the physical and emotional wreck that was Germany he described in a letter home as 'tragic', 'regardless of what one thinks of the earlier actions of the Germans'. Of course, he didn't want to ignore those 'earlier actions', as he recalled sixty years later before his German audience in Darmstadt: 'Because of the experiences of my own family and what we went through in the liberation of some concentration camps, there was a massive emotional gulf between Americans and the German population.'

On the other hand, Henry Kissinger was certain early on that any kind of common future could exist only if the 'image of the Germans as enemies' were overcome. One could not, he said in old age, treat the Germans as they had treated the Jews. So he ordered his people: 'Either we must let something positive come into being or we will always be administrators of chaos in this country; we are here because our values are superior to those of the Nazis.'

Incidentally, the gradual return to normal life had its good side, for the occupying forces as well. The theatres might have been unheated, but they went on playing, and Henry enjoyed his frequent trips to performances in Darmstadt and Heidelberg. He was particularly delighted with the resumption of the football season, which meant that he could attend the matches both of 1. FC Nürnberg and of his old club, Spielvereinigung Fürth.

July 1947 saw the end of the extra year for which he had volunteered. So, for the second time in nine years, Henry Kissinger turned his back on Germany, in a plane this time, and in the awareness that he would be seeing his old homeland again. Because he now knew that, in spite of everything, something bound him to the country.

Walter's situation was different, not least because he wasn't fighting in Europe. As an eighty-year-old he admitted that that had been his greatest disappointment during the war: he really wanted, he said, to make his contribution to bringing Nazi Germany to its knees. Walter had volunteered for the army and could hardly wait to get to the front. There was doubtless a certain thirst for adventure involved, but it wasn't the crucial factor. Walter thought it quite natural to defend the country that had given him and his family refuge at a most difficult time.

Like his brother Henry, with whom he continued to correspond during the war and the subsequent occupation, he too was first sent to a special army training programme, then joined the infantry, served in a supply unit in the Pacific, and was finally there when the 10th Army landed on Okinawa on 1 April

For the new homeland: Walter Kissinger as a young soldier in the American forces with his parents Louis and Paula.

1945. Three months later Admiral Nimitz announced the defeat of the Japanese resistance on the island, after a battle in which the US Army had suffered more casualties than in almost any other engagement of the Second World War.

Walter Kissinger, who had by now been promoted to the rank of captain, emerged unscathed, and was transferred with his unit to the occupying forces in Korea, where he was assigned to the military government. Here Colonel John C. Underwood took him under his wing. As his mentor, Underwood played a similar part for Walter to the one played by Fritz Kraemer in his brother's life. Underwood's influence is borne out by the fact that in 1967 Walter called his youngest son after him.

When Walter and John Kissinger visited Colonel Underwood shortly before his death, he gave his former subordinate and protégé a samurai sword that he had brought back from the Pacific War, to which John Kissinger still gives pride of place. Back then Underwood had engaged the twenty-one-year-old Walter in the reconstruction of the coal industry, which had declined under the Japanese occupation, which meant that the energy supply for the civilian population in the American-occupied zone of Korea was in the hands of Walter Kissinger for almost two years.

The period of occupation made a lasting impression on the young man, not least because it brought him into contact with the world of diplomacy. In his new function he was no longer a part of the army, but of the Foreign Service of the War Department. But above all he was excited about the big challenge that he now faced, and which he felt entirely a match for.

Looking back on his life, Walter later said in front of the camera that it was in the war, however terrible it might have been, that both brothers had to sit a kind of test, and that their military experience was a great help to both of them in finding their way in life.

It sparked a desire in Walter to have a senior professional

The diplomat: Walter Kissinger in Korea, after the end of the Second World War, mid-1940s.

post in civilian life too, one with a correspondingly high level of responsibility. By that standard, a life in New York's immigrant community would have amounted over time to a social decline. But first of all he went back there. Shortly before Christmas 1947 and a few months after his brother Henry, Walter, having been awarded the Decorated Commendation Medal, was home again.

His parents were happy that their two sons had survived the war, and unscathed at that. When Henry and Walter went to war, Louis and Paula were left alone with their worries. Their anxiety for their children was intensified by the news from Europe. It was bad enough that for years they hadn't been able to do anything for the family members left behind, but now reports were coming in that they, like so many people in their situation, initially did not want to believe. But then the information about extermination camps and gas chambers slowly turned into a brutal certainty.

The emotional burden was unbearable, and Louis more than anyone spent the war years in a state of depression. It was possible that that was why the pains in his abdominal region refused to go away, and even got worse. When the doctors finally diagnosed pancreatic cancer, Paula was close to despair. She had spent years looking after her husband, and now the care of the family rested on her shoulders alone. To make ends meet, and probably to keep from being lonely, she temporarily let a room in their apartment.

In 1945, when it became clear that an operation on his father was inevitable, Henry came home on leave for a few days to support his parents. The Irish doctor who performed the operation managed to save the sick man, and he also told his family he had good news for them: the cause of those years of pain was not cancer, but an inflammation of the gall bladder. So Louis Kissinger slowly began to convalesce, and by the time his sons came home he had largely recovered.

*

Henry Kissinger was twenty-four when he came back from Germany. Certainly, he had volunteered for an extra year, but for an ambitious man with academic ambitions, the war and the occupation amounted to wasted time. Henry was ambitious. In autumn 1947 he took up his studies at Harvard University. He initially studied governmental theory – a subject taught in that form only in America – as well as history, mathematics, French and chemistry, and, later, philosophy. But under the influence of William Yandell Elliott, who became his second great mentor after Fritz Kraemer, he soon concentrated entirely on governmental theory, and finished his studies with a monumental paper on 'The Significance of History'.

In February 1949, while he was writing this dissertation, Henry Kissinger married Anneliese Fleischer, whom he had met in the early 1940s. She was born in Nuremberg, in the immediate vicinity of Henry's home town of Fürth, before she and her family had also had to leave the country. Henry married this music- and literature-loving woman in his parents' apartment in Washington Heights, in the Orthodox Jewish style. The marriage collapsed in 1962. Two years later they divorced, but stayed in contact because of their children.

Elisabeth was born in 1959, and in 1961 a son called David, after Henry's paternal grandfather. Elisabeth later trained to be a doctor. David studied at New York University and Yale, working first as a journalist and lawyer before pursuing a career as a television producer, including a stint at Walt Disney Television, and ending up as president of Universal Television Productions. Elisabeth and David are now parents themselves, and Henry Kissinger is a proud grandfather of five.

When his children were born, Henry Kissinger was already at the peak of his first, academic career. He had laid the foundations for this immediately after completing his studies, and in

Proud: Henry Kissinger with his father Louis at his graduation ceremony in Harvard, 1954.

May 1954 was awarded a doctorate for his dissertation on the European state system after the defeat of Napoleon, which caused a furore and years later was published as a book, *The World Restored: Metternich, Castlereagh and the Problem of Peace, 1812–22*. But Henry would not be Henry if he wasn't undertaking a wealth of activities all at the same time Thus in 1952 he brought out his own journal, *Confluence*, in which he published articles by everyone who was anybody, or who soon would be.

But no initiatives were really of as much use to his further career as the Harvard International Seminar. With the help of his mentor Elliot, who was also director of the university summer school, Henry, who was still a graduate student, had since 1951 run this annual meeting of young careerists from all over the world. Until he moved to the White House in 1969, the seminar formed the core of his diverse activities. A whole generation of future presidents and prime ministers, foreign ministers, bankers and journalists were guests of Henry Kissinger in Cambridge, Massachusetts – an unparalleled network.

Even that wasn't enough for him. He wanted to go abroad, to Asia and Europe. In the summer of 1952 he went back to Germany, this time as a graduate student and director of the Harvard International Seminar. On the Rhine and the Ruhr, even though he himself hadn't yet turned thirty, he had meetings with representatives of German industry, which was just in the process of revival, and the fact that he sat around a table with some of them at Krupps, Germany's leading armaments manufacturer, prompted some ironic lines in a letter to his parents.

If Henry Kissinger was walking on familiar territory on his visits to Germany, on his trip to Asia he opened up fresh horizons. In 1951 the Operations Research Office sent him to Korea to investigate the influence of American troops on the civilian population. For the first time since the end of the Second World War, the United States had entered another war, although now on behalf of the United Nations, which had been founded in October 1945. In deciding to impose sanctions against North Korea and to set up a joint command under the leadership of the USA, the UN was responding to the attack by the communist North on the South of the peninsula, which launched the Korean War on 25 June 1950.

The attitude of the West was so resolute because North Korean units were wanting to take Seoul, the South Korean capital, and because in the capital cities of the West it was assumed that the Soviet Union and its dictator Josef Stalin were actually pulling the strings. In that respect, Korea was the first war between the free world and the communist world. By the time it finally ended, with a ceasefire that essentially re-established the status quo, more than three years had passed and there had been almost 160,000 American casualties, including the fallen, wounded, and those missing in action.

At first, hardly anyone had expected that – not even Walter Kissinger, who volunteered for service in Korea. Walter assumed that the Americans' involvement would be a limited police action, and he wanted to contribute the knowledge he had acquired during the occupation of Korea at the end of the war. But in the end he was not deployed, and, unlike his brother Henry, he didn't even enter the war arena. His disappointment was mitigated by the fact that he was able to continue his studies.

Having returned home from Korea at the end of 1947, Walter Kissinger followed John Underwood's advice, applied for a military grant and enrolled at the renowned Woodrow Wilson School of Public and International Affairs at Princeton University. All the students there have their eye on the diplomatic service, and that included Walter, who had enjoyed working in the Foreign Service of the War Department and was preparing for a career in the US Foreign Office.

In spring of 1951 he graduated as Bachelor of Arts with a dissertation on Russian policy in the Far East, 1895–1904. Korea wouldn't let go of him even now, because in the decade after the Sino-Japanese War discussed in Walter's dissertation, the international dispute over the country had played a crucial part. It comes as no surprise that Walter concluded his work, which was produced against the backdrop of the Korean War, with a contemporary perspective. It is his conclusions that startle the contemporary reader.

In 1951 Walter Kissinger wasn't just convinced that the Soviet policy of expansion was based less on ideological interests than on concrete political interests, he was also sure that in the long term the USA would have to drive a wedge between the two main communist powers, the Soviet Union and the People's Republic of China. At the time, more than half a million soldiers from Mao's People's Republic were fighting on the side of North Korea, and thus against America and her allies. In the early 1970s, when the USA actually started using the opposition between Moscow and Peking for its own interests, Walter's brother Henry was in charge of the American government's diplomacy.

Walter had long since turned to other horizons. As he was finishing his studies, the fear of communist infiltration was reaching its peak. In early 1950 the Republican senator Joseph R. McCarthy had claimed that more than two hundred communists had been identified in the State Department. Since then, the country had been swept by a wave of panic and hysteria. When some of Walter's fellow fighters from the occupation in Korea fell under suspicion, he had had enough.

Walter Kissinger bade goodbye to the idea of the Foreign Office, went to Harvard, where Henry's star was beginning to shine, graduated with an MBA from Harvard Business School in 1953, and quickly began to make a career for himself in the commercial world. Starting with a post as an executive assistant

*Close connection: Paula Kissinger with her daughter-in-law Genie,
Walter's wife, May 1989.*

*Party people: Paula Kissinger (right) and her husband Louis (third
from right) celebrating with their son Walter, daughter-in-law Genie
and their children at their home.*

in Ohio, he initially looked around in large companies, but couldn't find anything quite to his taste. Above all, the tendency to 'err on the side of caution' contradicted his entrepreneurial curiosity and his nature. Walter liked taking risks, in sport and in business.

In 1957, when he was given the opportunity to take over the troubled electrical company Advanced Vacuum Product, he leapt at the chance. At the time, the firm had a dozen employees and a turnover of US$50,000. When he left it four years later, he had overhauled the company, merged it with another, similar-sized operation, and increased the turnover more than two hundred-fold. At the age of thirty-eight, he was a made man, and Henry was, as Walter would put it in old age, 'known as my brother'.

Small wonder then, that he was able to pick and choose; and small wonder, too, that in the late sixties he was thinking about alternatives to a life in business. Possibilities up for debate were a return to private life, or else a return to public service as a diplomat. But as no real opportunities presented themselves, the world, as Walter later summed it up, with an ironic glance at his brother, 'was spared two Kissingers'.

One of the crucial experiences in Walter Kissinger's life was his meeting with Eugenie Van Drooge, known as 'Genie'. From a Dutch immigrant family, this young woman had studied philo-sophy, German and, principally, business studies at St Lawrence University, Canton, New York, had spent a year at Amsterdam University, and had graduated as a Bachelor of Arts. After practical years of apprenticeship – as a business consultant, for example – she crowned her studies with a qualification from the Radcliffe Program in Business Administration in Harvard, which is particularly notable for having been implemented before women were officially allowed to study at Harvard Business School.

On 4 July 1958, Eugenie Van Drooge and Walter Kissinger

married, secretly and alone. Both families were opposed to the liaison, because Genie was significantly younger than Walter, and was a Protestant to boot. 'Papa K.' and 'Mama K.' had particular problems with it. But then Paula Kissinger and her daughter-in-law soon formed a very close relationship. Even today, Genie speaks with the greatest warmth of Walter's mother, talks of her open nature and her ability to approach people without prejudice or arrogance, whatever their social status. Genie vividly remembers a scene when Paula, attending Henry Kissinger's award of an honorary knighthood, was sat next to Princess Diana at lunch and greeted her with the words, 'You're much prettier than you are in the photographs!'

Over the years, Genie's mother-in-law became her close confidante, her 'Wailing Wall'. Whenever Walter did something she didn't like, Genie would pour out her heart to Paula, who wouldn't hesitate to take her daughter-in-law's side: 'Give him back,' she would advise Genie, who still smiles when she tells that story. Paula, Genie said after her death, lives on not only in her memory and Walter's, but also in the memories of their children.

They had four children. Bill, their first, born in 1960, followed in his father's footsteps in that after studying governmental theory at Princeton and law at Berkeley, he spent some time in public service, first of all in the State Department during the Clinton administration, then as an assistant to the Governor of California. But in the end Bill carved out a career for himself, as a partner with a major law firm. John, Walter and Genie Kissinger's youngest child, born in 1967, has a whole series of university degrees under his belt, including qualifications from Princeton and Harvard. Like his wife, he is a keen actor and a passionate schoolteacher.

Dana, their daughter, who was born in 1964 and is, like her father, enthusiastic about sport, has the most international profile of Walter and Paula's children. Not only did she spend a year in

Golden wedding: Louis and Paula Kissinger celebrate their golden wedding in Switzerland in 1972. From left to right, back row: Genie and Walter Kissinger, Arno Kissinger, Louis's brother, Henry Kissinger with his children David and Elisabeth. Front, left to right: Paula and Louis Kissinger with his sister-in-law.

Geneva after studying Russian at university, she constantly travels the world for the International Bureau of Standards, and speaks several foreign languages fluently, including German. Her brothers' command of German is quite rudimentary, but they did learn their father's mother tongue because Walter thought it was important. That also brought them into contact with their grandmother's world – particularly Tom, Walter's second son, born in 1962. Professionally, Tom more than any of the other children has trodden in his father's footsteps, since he first studied history at Princeton, then business management at Harvard. Today he is on the board of a pharmaceutical company. As he grew older Tom became more and more interested in Paula's story. During the last years of her life he visited his grandmother regularly, usually once a week and usually on Friday for the Sabbath. After her death, Tom Kissinger ensured that the papers documenting the life of Paula and her family were safely preserved.

Of course, it wasn't all a bunch of roses in the Kissinger extended family. Paula couldn't get it into her head, for example, that her daughter-in-law wouldn't introduce Dana to the art of cooking. So Paula, who spent some time teaching her own family how to cook, set to work herself, but gave up after a few hours. 'You're right,' she said to Genie, 'it's not for her.'

Differences over the religious upbringing of the children were more serious, however. For Louis Kissinger it was unacceptable that Walter and Genie left questions of religious faith to the children themselves. As Paula said later, it broke his heart. She, too, had trouble with the idea, but tried to live with it as best she could, because the close connection with Walter, Genie and the children was important to her.

For Louis Kissinger, his faith had lost none of its power over the years and decades, but had actually grown in importance. In the

At the peak: Henry Kissinger (right) with his children David (front right) and Elisabeth (seated, right) and brother Walter and his children John (second from left) and Dana in the Swiss mountains near Laax, 1972.

bad, almost desperate days, it was an unquenchable source of hope and confidence, and since living in America his faith had also become a bridge to the past. If there was anything that bound him intellectually, spiritually and emotionally to his old homeland, it was his firm anchoring in that faith; it was there that it had been taught to him, there that it had come to maturity. And if there was a place where that could be felt, it was by the graves of his ancestors.

His sons recognized that and persuaded their parents, partly for that very reason, to visit Germany shortly after the war. That called for a great deal of tact and patience. Louis and Paula Kissinger had lost many of their closest relatives during the German campaign to exterminate European Jewry, and Louis in particular was burdened by the memory that he had not been able to do anything to save his three sisters from deportation and death. But they eventually gave in to their sons' pleading, and in 1952 Louis and Paula Kissinger took their first major trip to Europe, to visit their relatives' graves.

At least, those graves that could be found: most of the members of the Kissinger and Stern families had been deported to Izbica, and from there probably sent to the gas chambers of Sobibor or Belzec. So the Jewish cemeteries of Bechhofen, Ermershausen and Fürth became the places to which Louis, Paula, Henry and Walter Kissinger returned when they were in their old homeland. Since the Jewish community of Leutershausen did not have a cemetery of its own, like other surrounding communities they buried their dead in the Jewish cemetery north-west of Bechhofen, which had been laid out at the end of the sixteenth century. The grave of Peppi Stern, Paula's mother, was there as well.

In the Jewish cemetery of Ermershausen, which dates from the middle of the eighteenth century, Karolina Kissinger, Louis's mother, found her final resting place, and Falk Stern is buried in the new Jewish cemetery in Fürth. Because the old graveyard, which opened in 1607, reached its limits towards the end of the nineteenth century, the Jews of Fürth were given an additional site on Erlanger Strasse. It is here that Falk Stern's plain grave lies. It became the central place at which Louis and Paula Kissinger and their sons remembered the dead.

Of course, Louis and Paula, when they came to Germany in 1952, didn't just visit their ancestors' graves. They also wanted to see the people who had always stood by them in the difficult times leading up to their flight. The connection with the Hezners was never broken, and most recently had been maintained chiefly by Henry. Now Louis and Paula came to Leutershausen. It was their first visit since their expulsion, and it was important. The sons saw that quite clearly.

From now on, the trips to Europe, and to Germany, were no longer an impossible obstacle; but they didn't like coming. In fact, it was only contact with the Hezners that brought Louis and Paula, sometimes accompanied by one of their sons, on their occasional visits to Fürth and Leutershausen. Otherwise, they avoided the place 'that had once been home', as it reads on one of the photographs from those years.

Although they used to spend their summers in Switzerland – and the winters in Puerto Rico, because their son Walter was often there on business – Louis and Paula didn't return to their former home until 1975. Karl and Babby Hezner, and also their two daughters, with their families, often went to Flims in the Swiss mountains to meet up with Paula and Louis Kissinger. On one occasion the families met in Germany: towards the end of August 1972, at Stuttgart railway station.

Walter often travelled to Germany as well, later because his business took him there. It was similar for Henry. His professional activities brought him there more and more often during the 1950s. Like his parents, his brother and his uncle

Among friends: Henry Kissinger with his first wife Anne in the 1950s with the Hezner family in his grandfather Falk Stern's old garden in Leutershausen. Left to right: Willy Häffner, Erika Bickert, Henry Kissinger, Lore Häffner, 'Babby' Hezner, Anne Kissinger, Karl Hezner. At the front: the grandchildren of Babby and Karl Hezner.

Karl, he too visited Ermershausen on one occasion during this time; but above all, throughout this period, he used the opportunity of work-related visits to Germany to make occasional side-trips to Leutershausen.

Once he went there with his wife Anne, to show her the place where he had spent his childhood. But he never set foot inside it again. Unlike Walter, who liked to take a close look at the family home, Henry kept his distance; he preferred to study his grandparents' property from the window of the town hall opposite. After the late 1950s such visits were out of the question, because as a very busy man he could no longer find the time, and because his footsteps were followed with interest by the public, including the German public.

That had been the case in America since the mid-1950s. It was with an essay published by Henry Kissinger in the spring 1955 issue of *Foreign Affairs*, a journal that gave impetus to many a career, that he made his breakthrough. His work, which set against the current nuclear strategy of massive retaliation the concept of a locally limited, 'small' nuclear war, brought Henry Kissinger a number of offers.

Among these were two from noted universities, which he refused, and one from the renowned Council on Foreign Relations in New York, which he accepted. Henry ran the study group on Nuclear Weapons and Foreign Policy there from 1955, concluding his work with the publication of a book of the same name, which became a best-seller and put him on the front page of the *New York Times*. In his mid-thirties he was suddenly a made man.

By now the young star had also come to the attention of Nelson Aldrich Rockefeller. The son of the oil magnate John D. Rockefeller Jr, one of President Dwight D. Eisenhower's foreign policy advisers, appointed him in the spring of 1956 as director of a study project and, when it was completed, took him on as a freelance adviser. After Fritz Kraemer and William Elliot, Henry

Kissinger found his third sponsor in Nelson Rockefeller. Until he went to Nixon in 1969, he had this well-paid adviser's post, and with it a second string to his bow, alongside his university career, to which he had returned after completing his work with the Council on Foreign Relations. From 1959 he was associate professor, and from 1962 full professor, at Harvard.

In the late 1950s, Henry Kissinger made a name for himself far beyond the world of academia, in America and also in Germany. Over the next few years he was a frequent guest there. It was far from obvious that that should have happened. There were emigrants who would never set foot on German soil again, let alone build up an intense relationship with the country and even go so far as to accept its honours and awards.

Henry Kissinger's case was different, because he was ambitious and saw in his German roots an opportunity for a career, because in his later political offices it was impossible for him to stay out of Germany, and because in his own way he had dealt with what had happened, without forgetting it. Whenever he spoke in Germany over the coming years he said nothing, aside from the odd remark, about the injustice and pain that had once been inflicted on him.

'I grew up in Germany in painful circumstances. Nonetheless, in spite of the trauma of those years I have always felt a deep affection for the country of my youth.' And he never said anything more than he did now in Aachen, when he was awarded the International Charlemagne Prize at the end of May 1987. No accusations, no condemnation. Just the plea that everyone should work together to make sure that nothing like that ever happened again, anywhere.

That was remarkable, and far from guaranteed. There were others who had, like Henry, suffered great injustices in Germany, people who had only just managed to get out of the country as children, people who had gone on to carve great careers for themselves in America. Some of these could not resist wagging a raised finger, to prick a national conscience and play upon a permanent, subliminal sense of reproach, probably knowing that no opposition to the gesture was likely to be forthcoming from the Federal Republic.

Henry Kissinger unconditionally resisted that temptation, if he was ever aware of it at all. Of course, with his reputation and qualifications he could have got a hearing in Germany at any time. Even so, the decision was noteworthy. Perhaps that self-imposed limitation, that consistent abstention from backward-looking condemnation, was also the reason why he was able to return to the country after the disaster.

In January 1959, at the invitation of the foreign minister, Heinrich von Brentano, Henry Kissinger spent three weeks travelling through the Federal Republic. On his schedule were the cities of Düsseldorf, Berlin, Hamburg, Frankfurt, Koblenz, Bonn, Munich and, as a side-trip, Fürth. It wasn't the first time since he was a sergeant in the American army of occupation that the thirty-five-year-old had come to Franconia. But unlike on his previous visits, he was now a famous man. 'Professor Henry A. Kissinger, 35, Associate Director of the Center for International Affairs at Harvard University, author of books and articles on history and politics, adviser to US policy makers and the US military, inventor of the "limited war" in the nuclear age, born in Fürth', as the *Fürther Nachrichten* described him, stayed for a day, honoured the city council with his visit, attended the Stadttheater in the evening, and went on record as saying: 'I think some of the influence that I was able to gain in the USA is due to the fact that my youth granted me the perspective of a different world.'

So, Henry knew that his biography was a gift, if he knew how to use it. That did not stop with that visit to Germany, even though he wouldn't see Fürth again for a long time. In May 1961, when the Berlin crisis was coming to a head, he was back in Bonn, this time on an official mission. The American president, John F. Kennedy, had sent him to the city on the Rhine to hold discussions with Konrad Adenauer.

The old first Chancellor of the Federal Republic didn't think much of the young intellectuals around the equally young US president, but he was thoroughly charmed by this 'Professor Kissinger'. Even though he was less than forty, he showed that he thought Adenauer was the 'greatest German statesman since Bismarck' – as he wrote in the early 1990s – and naturally the old gentleman was very pleased. The emissary was also able to explain the complicated US nuclear strategy to the Chancellor both competently and in his own language. Of course, Adenauer accepted it.

But then it turned out that while Henry's German was good enough for discussing football, it wasn't quite up to specialist nuclear questions, so an interpreter was brought in. After Kissinger had left, when the interpreter gave the old man the minutes of the discussion, Adenauer told him to destroy them. He had promised his guest that nothing about his linguistic difficulties would be leaked to the outside world. Twenty years later, the interpreter told Henry the story, and he himself made it public in 1998 when he was in Germany again and – in Fürth and in rather stumbling German – expressing his thanks for his honorary citizenship.

During the 1950s and 1960s Henry Kissinger repeatedly wanted to travel to Germany for one reason or another. During the 1970s he had to visit his old homeland more or less regularly, in an official function. When the new president, Richard Nixon, took office, Henry entered the leading echelon of American politics. He remained there until Nixon's successor, Gerald Ford, cleared the White House. This did not necessarily go without saying, because Nixon and Kissinger had never met before the president assumed power. For many years Henry Kissinger had been an adviser and confidant to Nelson Rockefeller, Nixon's rival in the Republican Party. The fact that Nixon now brought him in says something for the reputation that preceded the professor.

For eight years, from 20 January 1969 until 20 January 1977, the German-born Jewish immigrant occupied the control centres of American world power. Until November 1975, Henry Kissinger held the office of National Security Adviser, which he filled like no one before him, and hardly anyone since. If William Rogers, the Secretary of State, was lucky, he was told what the president and his security adviser – in many cases using means of secret diplomacy – had prepared or already put into action. In September 1973, when Rogers wearily threw in the towel, Henry became Secretary of State. He was the fifty-sixth Secretary of State of the United States, and the first not to be born in the country.

The 'whole Kissinger clan', as his mother put it, was there when he swore his oath on 22 September 1973. His parents knew the Washington scene. They had last been there in January, on the occasion of the formal inauguration of President Nixon. Henry had insisted on going through a busy schedule with his parents; he had introduced them not only to many of the members of the administration, to senators and congressmen, but also to stars of American journalism, not least Barbara Walters, an intimate friend, and to show-business personalities. So Louis and Paula Kissinger had met Bob Hope, Pat Boone, and, at a party in his house, Frank Sinatra.

No question about it, Henry was a star – and, like all stars, he had to pay for his status. On his way to the summit of power he had used the press – he had played with journalists, as Marvin Kalb, one of his ablest biographers, puts it. Now the media played with him: they used his name to fill their gossip columns. Everything he did was exposed to the curious eyes of the public. At Christmas 1972 the American book market was deluged with all kinds of new publications about Henry Kissinger. Souvenir shops sold Kissinger figures, and the latest thing was a 'Super Kiss Watch', a larger-than-life watch with a Swiss mechanism and a red, blue and white armband.

But the big subject of those months was: Henry and women. The Nuremberg *Abendzeitung*, which kept Henry's Franconian compatriots up to date, summed things up at the end of 1973: 'Today the television star Marlo Thomas, tomorrow the scandal-drenched Mamie van Doren, tomorrow the super-intelligent Jill St John, then Margaret Osmer, television producer, or Nancy Maginnes, political adviser to Governor Rockefeller, and Candice Bergen, actress, and, and, and . . . Women are his hobby. But when does he actually have time for it?' Quite. But such stories are actually part of being a real star, particularly an American one. The truth of the matter is neither here nor there.

From the end of 1973 a lady started popping up more and more often in the reports, and even the *Abendzeitung* asked, 'Is Henry Kissinger going to get hitched today?' And indeed he did, although not in December 1973. Nancy Maginnes was a striking, confident, tall character. At five foot nine inches, the green-eyed, blonde chain-smoker with the rather long face clearly towered over her husband, eleven years her senior. She had studied history, graduated from Berkeley, and then worked for Nelson Rockefeller. It was there that the two of them had met in the mid-sixties. On 30 March 1974, Henry and Nancy were married, not far from Washington airport, at dead of night. They went on a short honeymoon to Acapulco with Walter and Genie, undiscovered at first by the press.

Of course, the hubbub surrounding Henry didn't escape the attention of his parents. They had lived in America too long to

On honeymoon: Henry Kissinger with his second wife Nancy Maginnes after their wedding in Acapulco, Mexico, March 1974.

be surprised by it. Besides, they knew their son, and knew or guessed what was true in the reports about his relationships with women, and what wasn't. At any rate, Nancy, when Louis and Paula Kissinger were in Washington for Nixon's inauguration, was of the party, as 'Mama K.' wrote in a long letter to Arno Kissinger and his family. On that occasion they had travelled from New York by train, the Metroliner.

Now, in September 1973, a day before their son's formal swearing-in, they came by plane, because on this occasion they were exhausted by an interrupted trip to Switzerland, and because, as strictly observant Jews, they couldn't travel on a Saturday. Two days later, Walter, Genie and their four children arrived, as did Henry's children, David and Elisabeth, whom they called 'Lizzie'. Walter organized a dinner for them all, and on this occasion Paula noticed how much David admired his father and how much, unlike his sister, he loved being in the spotlight.

The next day, in the East Room of the White House, the big moment came. There were lots of people there: deputies and senators, the president and many administration officials, but also former sponsors of Henry's like Nelson Rockefeller and Fritz Kraemer, as well as prominent people like Kirk Douglas. His mother held the Bible as her son swore his oath, and saw tears in his eyes.

Back in New York, when she put her 'thoughts of a mother on the occasion of the swearing-in of her son as Secretary of State' on paper, she didn't know how to capture her feelings in words. They would best, she wrote in English, be described by the German word 'Demut', meaning 'humility': 'Why were we chosen to have a son to occupy this position? Was it God's will that Henry should take part in the construction of a better world? Did we simple people do anything to get him where he is? It's possible that Henry's deep affection for us answers the question.

The big day: Henry Kissinger is sworn in as American Secretary of State. His mother Paula holds the Bible, 22 September 1973.

Standing for the family photo. Left to right: Henry Kissinger's son David (hidden), Henry Kissinger, his daughter Elisabeth, Paula Kissinger, Louis Kissinger, Walter's son Tom Kissinger, President Richard Nixon, Walter Kissinger, Genie Kissinger. Front: Walter's youngest children John and Dana.

There wasn't an important event in his life that he didn't share with us.'

When their son brought his parents to the airport in a limousine and told his mother how proud he had been of her 'dignified attitude', Paula Kissinger took it as the 'highest accolade that a mother could ever receive'. Even during the moving ceremony in the White House, she knew that Henry 'would never change, that regardless of his huge success he would always remain the elegant, sensitive person he had been when he set off on his journey'. Moving and moved words, certainly: but why shouldn't a mother capture on paper something of which she is convinced?

At any rate, she had no more illusions than her son. 'If my origins can contribute anything to the formulation of policy,' he had said during the ceremony, 'then it is this: I saw at an early age what can happen to a society that is based on hatred, strength and suspicion.' Henry Kissinger never forgot his origins; and his origins would never let him go – not even when he was at the peak of his career.

Henry Kissinger's achievements in the eight years that he spent at the centre of power are beyond dispute. Among the greatest of them was the facilitation of a truce in Vietnam, even if it was accompanied by a late radicalization of American warfare in south-east Asia. This included the intensification of military measures against North Vietnam, alongside the mining of the coastal waters, heavy bombing raids on military and civilian targets, and the temporary invasion of Cambodia. Hanoi, Kissinger said years later, justifying these actions, which had drawn international criticism, 'only negotiated when they came under severe pressure'.

It wasn't just in the negotiations over a truce in Vietnam that Henry Kissinger opted for methods 'that you wouldn't find in a

Thoughts of a Mother on the Swearing in of her son as Secretary of State.

When we started out on our trip to Washington on Sept. 21, there were the words of the Man of La Mancha in my ears - "this was the impossible dream."

Was it really true that Henry had been confirmed as Secretary of State, the first Jew the first foreign born, our son? Was it still possible - the American success story - that from humble beginnings, from years of hard work and dedication, one could rise to this position. It did strengthen the belief in a better world, in which still hopes and ideals exist, in spite of disappointments and let downs.

We flew this time not because we felt as VIP's, but because we were

A mother's thoughts: Paula Kissinger records her thoughts and feelings on the occasion of her son Henry's swearing in as Secretary of State of the United States of America, September 1973.

textbook', and for a few years he helped secret diplomacy to blossom again. So the public did not learn until late in January 1972, for example, that for two years the security adviser had been negotiating a truce with Le Duc Tho, the North Vietnamese representative, in Paris. It was signed a year later, and the same year both men were awarded the Nobel Peace Prize.

America's withdrawal from Vietnam became possible because North Vietnam's two most important allies neutralized one another: in March 1969 the rivalry that had been fermenting for years between the Soviet Union and the People's Republic of China along the east Asian Ussuri River ended in a massive military confrontation. The conditions were in place for the implementation of a diplomatic strategy that Walter Kissinger, who had originally wanted to go into the diplomatic service, had proposed in the spring of 1951. In his Princeton dissertation on Russian policy in the Far East between 1895 and 1904, the younger of the two brothers had reached the conclusion that American diplomacy should use the conflict between the two leading communist powers for its own purposes, to drive a wedge between them in the long term.

That was exactly what Henry did – even though he didn't know his brother's work, and had never taken an interest in Walter's early thoughts – twenty years later.

In July 1971, as Nixon's security adviser he entered into secret negotiations in the People's Republic of China and, with prime minister Chou En-Lai, prepared for the president's spectacular visit to Peking. In February 1972 Nixon spent almost a week in communist China, laid the groundwork for the acceptance of diplomatic relations, and thus put the Soviets under pressure.

Then, when the president travelled to Moscow in May 1972, he was also able to reap a harvest there, one for which the seeds had been sown by his security adviser. For months – sometimes officially, sometimes confidentially – Henry Kissinger had been

Lost in concentration: Henry Kissinger, Secretary of State of the USA 1973–77.

dealing with the Soviets, so that Richard Nixon was finally able to sign a series of treaties with Leonid Brezhnev, the strong man in the Kremlin, the most important of them being SALT I, at the time a pioneering agreement for a limitation of strategic nuclear weapons.

Then, from autumn 1973, the Middle East was top of the agenda. Henry Kissinger, by now Secretary of State, travelled to the region eleven times between October 1973 and August 1975. The goal of this shuttle diplomacy was an approach to Israel and its Arab neighbours after the Yom Kippur War. In fact, the Separation of Forces Agreement that Israel and Egypt signed in January 1974 was the beginning of a difficult but in some ways entirely successful peace process.

Someone who travelled a lot with Henry in those days calculated that in his time as Secretary of State alone, a period of three years and two months, he had taken forty-one foreign trips, covering far over half a million miles, an average of 15,000 miles per month. Of course the fifty-nine countries he visited included the Federal Republic of Germany. Henry travelled to the country nine times between March 1974 and September 1976, as Secretary of State. This is a relatively large number of visits, and has something to do with the fact that presidents were hardly ever seen in Bonn: neither Nixon nor Ford made a single state visit to the city on the Rhine.

That wasn't because of bad relations with their German partners; quite the reverse; just as Gerald Ford would later have a good relationship with Helmut Schmidt after Nixon's resignation in August 1974, Richard Nixon and Willy Brandt, Schmidt's predecessor, got on very well with one another, all in all. Nixon and Brandt were both born in 1913, were both self-made men, and had little option but to stand shoulder to shoulder. They were mutually dependent.

If the US was to compromise with the Soviet Union, as it needed to do after the withdrawal from Vietnam, it would have been very useful if the German Chancellor were to acknowledge the fact that Germany was permanently divided. If that were to happen, America wouldn't have to work so hard for reunification. Brandt in turn couldn't implement his eastern policy or his policy on Germany without, let alone against, Nixon. In particular, for agreement to be reached between the four victorious powers over Berlin, he needed the Americans. Besides, where the security of the Federal Republic was concerned, nothing had changed: it was and remained dependent on the United States, one-sidedly and unconditionally. So if the Chancellor voiced any criticism of the American war in Vietnam or the Nixon administration's brutal economic protection policy, he did so behind closed doors.

Much the same could be said of the American president and his security adviser. Publicly, they gave an appropriate welcome to the German Chancellor, who paid five official visits to the United States. But what they really thought about their visitor was recorded in secret tape recordings in the Oval Office. Nixon and Kissinger agreed on the 'main problem': Brandt 'wasn't very bright'. In fact, he was 'a bit stupid', and also, according to Kissinger, 'he drinks'. Nonetheless, Brandt seemed to 'be behaving himself' and to understand that he owed them both 'a whole lot'.

In fact, such disrespect should come as a surprise, because not only did Nixon's and Brandt's careers reveal similarities, but Kissinger's biography and that of Brandt, ten years his senior, at least had the big break in common: they had both had to leave Germany at a young age to escape the Nazis. In August 1938, when Henry Kissinger went to the United States, Willy Brandt had already been in Scandinavia for almost five and a half years, first in Oslo and later, after the German invasion of Norway, in Stockholm. So for a few years Willy Brandt lived in the city in which Henry's grandfather David Kissinger and his son, Henry's uncle Arno, had found refuge.

Moreover, like Henry Kissinger, Willy Brandt also initially returned to Germany in a foreign uniform – one in an American uniform, the other in a Norwegian one. But unlike Henry Kissinger, who emigrated later and made America his home, Willy Brandt, who had fled Germany as early as April 1933, stayed in his old homeland after he returned. Could that have been a reason for certain disagreements between the two men, some of them plainly matters of atmosphere, the 'shadows' that sometimes 'haunted' their relations, as Brandt put it? Hardly likely.

Instead, it lay in their very different characters and, at least at first, in mutual misunderstandings about each other's actual or supposed intentions. We can only understand that if we are aware of Henry's deep-rooted respect for the weight and capabilities of Germany and the Germans. Respect is not far removed from fear. Even years after the end of the Cold War and the unification of Germany, he wrote that 'not even ... defeat in the Second World War' could 'diminish ... Germany's influence in the world'. No one who had experienced the horrendous abuse of that influence in the 1930s could be pleased about that.

In the fat book of memoirs that he committed to paper after leaving the State Department, Henry Kissinger reveals what it was that he distrusted about the foreign policy of the new liberal-socialist coalition: 'It seemed to me', he wrote in 1979, 'that Brandt's new *Ostpolitik*, which looked to many like a progressive policy of quest for détente, could in less scrupulous hands turn into a new form of classic German nationalism.' It says much for Kissinger that he later saw this view of things as a mistake and publicly corrected himself, just as in retrospect Brandt did not withhold his 'admiration' for Kissinger's 'great gifts'. But by that time both of them had left office long before.

When they still held those offices, the two men seldom communicated directly. On the difficult question of Berlin above all,

Egon Bahr, secretary of state in the Chancellor's office, was the man with whom Kissinger had most dealings. Admittedly he didn't entirely trust Brandt's 'extraordinarily skilful intermediary', but he did hold him in high esteem, because Bahr was able to communicate with Kissinger through his favourite channel, secrecy. But that did little to change the atmospheric disturbances in German–American relations during those years.

The Germans had their problems with the Americans because the Americans had problems all over the world, and they weren't willing or able to pay any heed to the Germans, who depended upon them. One crucial cause for transatlantic irritation lay in the USA's balance of payments and trade deficit, for which, more than anything else, the high costs of the Vietnam War were responsible. The collapse of the dollar led to a flight into foreign currencies, particularly the German mark, and finally, in August 1971, to unilateral measures on the part of the American government. Without even informing their allies, the international currency system was suspended overnight.

Something of the kind had been in the air for some time, because the foreign reserves of US$50 billion were only covered to about 20 per cent by American gold reserves. So in fact there was little to object to in the decision. But what caused annoyance and irritation in European capitals was the imperial style of the American policy, and that was linked with the name of Henry Kissinger. And he added insult to injury.

On 23 April 1973, the security adviser sent a message to the Europeans. In it – with a discreet reference to the indispensable protection of the USA – he distinguished their regional interests from the global interests of the USA, and recommended that they adapt to the concept of the American superpower. Still, Kissinger conceded to the Europeans – in what would soon come to be known as his Easter message – that America would 'never knowingly sacrifice ... or harm the interests of others'. It wasn't just cynicism, it was also the certainty that Europe would sooner or later have to come to its senses and adapt to the rules of the American game.

And that was what happened, more quickly than expected. On 6 October 1973, the Jewish festival of Yom Kippur, when Egypt and Syria launched a surprise attack on Israel and thus started the fourth Middle East war, America showed who was in charge, both at home and abroad. Without informing the German government, let alone consulting them, the Americans used their military depots and bases in the Federal Republic, such as Bremerhaven, to supply the Israelis with military equipment and thus support their war effort. A furious Chancellor Willy Brandt was informed that the Federal Republic now had 'only limited sovereignty'. Washington 'reserved the right to adopt measures which appeared appropriate and necessary in the interests of international security'.

Throughout all of his working life Henry Kissinger had been a pragmatist. For the American security adviser and Secretary of State that meant: everything is subordinate to American interests in the narrower or the wider sense, including partnerships and, if such things can be said to exist in politics at all, friendships. There was no room for sentimental memories or affections. If Germany still had a particular part to play in Henry Kissinger's thoughts and feelings, he would certainly grant it no room in his daily business.

There were other forums for that. It is interesting that Henry made use of them to show his special relationship with Germany. That he made use of them when he was at the peak of his political career is remarkable. That he documented that special relationship with Germany in Fürth, the place of his birth, says a great deal about the man's relationship with his first home and the city of his childhood and early youth.

On 7 June 1973, in a closed session, Fürth city council

decided to award Henry Kissinger the Citizen's Gold Medal. Henry accepted the invitation to the ceremony. But the council had to wait patiently for two and a half years before a date could finally be found, with the active participation of the Foreign Office – and then only because of a change of Cabinet in Madrid, which unexpectedly opened up a large hole in Kissinger's busy calendar. The long hesitation is partially explained by the increasingly heavy workload to which Henry had been exposed since being appointed Secretary of State.

Besides, the great crisis of the Nixon administration, the Watergate scandal, didn't leave the president's right-hand man unscathed. It was sparked in June 1972 by a burglary of the headquarters of the Democratic Party, which was based at the time in the Watergate complex in Washington. Who can tell what might have happened if the president, once it had leaked out and become the burning issue in the *Washington Post*, hadn't become involved in all kinds of attempted cover-up operations. But although the strangeness and incongruities accumulated over time, although a Senate committee undertook its investigation of the presidential election campaign in front of millions of television viewers, at first Nixon couldn't really be touched. He went on protesting his innocence.

It wasn't until mid-July 1973 that the president, as he always did, recorded on tape his discussions with the men responsible for the burglary and the scandal that followed. In connection with a series of further scandals and resignations, including that of Nixon's vice president, Spiro T. Agnew, and his justice minister, Elliott L. Richardson, the president came under such pressure that, in late April 1974, he had to produce a transcript, albeit a heavily edited one, of the tapes. With the threat of dismissal in front of him, on the evening of 8 August, Nixon announced his resignation for the following day. He was the first president of the United States to take such a step.

In the summer of 1974 Henry Kissinger was also caught up

in the shock waves of the political earthquake in Washington. In the middle of June, at a press conference in far-off Salzburg, he suddenly and violently threatened his immediate resignation if the campaign unleashed against him in connection with Watergate was not stopped straightaway. And at the end of July the question of whether his days were numbered as Secretary of State was aired all around the world. But it didn't come to that.

Henry Kissinger survived the earthquake and Nixon's resignation, stayed in office, and thus ensured continuity in the transition to the brief Ford era. That all took energy and time. There was no time to think of the Citizen's Gold Medal waiting for him in Fürth. And who knows when he would have accepted it if the Spanish Cabinet hadn't been reshuffled, leading to that unexpected gap in his calendar.

Henry didn't travel alone. He used the opportunity for a family reunion, because his brother and parents had also come to Fürth for this occasion. It wasn't the first visit since Louis and Paula Kissinger had had to leave the city. In the 1950s they had visited occasionally – for the first time in 1952, to visit the grave of Paula's father, Falk Stern, and to see the Hezners again. But now, late in 1975, the Kissingers – Louis, Paula, Henry and Walter – met up at home, together as a family for the first time since their expulsion.

Both participants and observers knew that Henry's honouring was the reason, but perhaps not the only one, perhaps not even the real reason for the trip. The local press did establish that the Citizen's Gold Medal had been 'awarded to the famous Henry', but was 'doubtless also conceived of as a moral compensation for his elderly parents'. And in retrospect *Der Spiegel* summed everything up in these terms: 'Henry was by no means the main person ... That was his father Louis Kissinger, almost 90 years old.'

The parents had already arrived the previous day, in the company of the German ambassador to Washington, Berndt von Staden. When Paula looked back on the event more than two decades later, shortly before her death, she said, 'It was unreal. The government sent limousines. A lady from the Foreign Office was detailed to us. First you're exiled, and then you're treated like a royal highness. It was unreal. But I was happy to be there.'

Henry came on 15 December, a cold, sunny Monday, with Nancy on board the Boeing 707. In fact, the two of them were only making a short side-trip on the way from an American ambassadors' conference in London to an energy conference in Paris. The Secretary of State spent a whole six hours in the city of his birth. But the expenditure was enormous. The protocol organized by the Foreign Office and the security measures established by the American government left no room for manoeuvre.

The Bavarian minister of state for the interior had ordered the implementation of security stage II, and the order issued by Nuremberg/Fürth police headquarters did not rule out 'a threat or disturbance', 'from abstract sources'. Basically, the fear was that 'visits by political representatives of the USA to the Federal Republic – in particular Minister Kissinger' would be taken by certain left-wing groups 'as a reason to use actions to draw attention to their organization and its aims'. Apart from his own troop of American security officials, some four hundred German police were mobilized. By the reckoning of the local press, those were 'just as many as tend to be deployed for visits by Willy Brandt'. The armoured Mercedes 600 had been flown in the previous day, and during the visit helicopters were constantly circling above the places where the city's guest happened to be.

Luckily there were no incidents. The visit was a great success, and for a brief moment Fürth was at the centre of international interest: 'Kissinger visits his home town to great applause' read the headline in the *New York Times*. And hundreds of people in

The homecomers: Henry, Walter, Paula and Louis Kissinger in Fürth, 15 December 1975.

Fürth were on their feet when the motorcade with their prominent guest drove into the city from Nuremberg airport.

There were 400 guests in the solemnly decorated Stadt-theater, among them the Bavarian prime minister Alfons Goppel, Bonn's foreign minister Hans-Dietrich Genscher, and also the American ambassador to Bonn and the German ambassador to Washington, Martin J. Hillenbrand and Berndt von Staden. Some people who couldn't be present at the party, like former Chancellor Ludwig Erhard, probably the most famous son of the city of Fürth and father of the German economic miracle, wrote their guest of honour some nice lines 'in memory of so many fruitful discussions'. Gustav Schickedanz was there as well. The head of the Quelle mail-order company was also a holder of the Citizen's Gold Medal, and (like Max Grundig, who was disabled) an embodiment of that same economic miracle and one of the city's showcase entrepreneurs. Twenty years later, at the celebration of mail-order king Schickedanz's hundredth birthday, Henry was back in Fürth to deliver the official address.

Today he spoke in English, but then delivered the German translation himself. His speech was short, statesmanlike, and filled with fundamental reflections. Only at one point, close to the beginning, did he become personal, and some listeners had the impression that his voice threatened to fail for a moment. 'I am particularly pleased', he said in the city of his childhood and early adolescence, 'that I can spend this day of honour in the presence of my family, especially my parents, who have never abandoned their connections to this city, in which they spent the greatest part of their lives.'

The reporter from the *Nürnberger Nachrichten*, who followed the spectacle in Fürth, Nuremberg's neighbour and rival, with a mocking undertone, recognized the emotional dimension of the moment: 'If there was anything moving about this brief flying visit by a busy diplomatic star, it was the loving and respectful father–son relationship.' And it almost seemed to the observer 'as if it was above all the bond with the old father, and with the still agile mother, that allowed him to find a gap in his packed schedule for the trip to Fürth.'

After the ceremony the Kissingers went to the canteen of the city savings bank to restore their strength. On the menu, along with Franconian bratwursts, were chicken drumsticks, smoked fish and roast beef. Of course, their hosts also provided a table of kosher delicacies such as fish, egg dishes and cheese. Then Franconian wine, Franconian beer and other drinks were served, and as Paula addressed her scotch on the rocks, her daughter-in-law Nancy sipped from a glass of milk.

The bank canteen was chosen because the nine-storey building, in the seventies concrete style, was easy to secure, and above all because from its top floor one has a wonderful view of the whole of Fürth. So the canteen view replaced the tour of the city that had originally been planned, and which had to be abandoned because of the tight timetable, but above all because of the intervention of the security services.

From up there the Kissingers' eyes wandered along the streets of their old home, lingered here and there, at 5 Marienstrasse, for example, where they had lived for fifteen years, or the exposed fortress of the Alte Veste, where Heinz and Walter used to cycle. Henry was visibly lost in dreams. If he spoke to his mother in German on this occasion, it was probably out of politeness to his hosts.

They then handed over their presents – to Henry, but also to his father. The mayor of Ermershausen, who had been present at the ceremony at the express wish of Louis Kissinger, gave Henry's parents not only a pewter plate, but also the gramophone record 'Ermershausen', with a picture of Louis Kissinger's birthplace.

The new bearer of the Citizen's Gold Medal was showered with gifts. The head of Spielvereinigung Fürth pinned the club's gold badge to the beaming guest's lapel and handed him a

*A safe distance: Henry Kissinger and his parents look for
5 Marienstrasse, the house in which the family lived until their
emigration in 1938. On the right in the picture: Fürth's mayor Kurt
Scherzer, 15 December 1975.*

'golden football boot'. In return, Henry had to sign no fewer than twenty club pennants. He hardly managed to put his pen down. After he had given one of the city councillors his autograph, a regular autograph frenzy broke out among the hundred or so guests: 'It's always like that,' the patient guest of honour commented, 'once you've started . . .'

The mayor of the city of Fürth gave him a carefully chosen book: Exodus, the second volume of the five books of the Jewish Pentateuch, printed in 1802 by David Zirndorfer. At the head of the title page the book shows the coat of arms of Fürth in the claws of the Prussian eagle, thus recalling the brief period between 1792 and 1806 when Fürth belonged to Prussia. They weren't the city's worst years. Henry Kissinger knew the meaning of the present, and followed up his official thank-you letter, which he wrote at the end of December, with a second one expressing his profound gratitude.

Then, when Louis Kissinger spoke, you could have heard a pin drop up there in that sterile, utilitarian bank building. The old man had carefully prepared his speech at home, and written it down on paper by hand. Paula talked to Walter and asked him to ensure that her husband could deliver his speech. Walter took control of the matter; and some other aspects of the arrangements, such as his father's meeting with his former pupils, likewise fell to the younger of the two Kissinger brothers. The trip had an emotional quality of its own for Walter as well. He hadn't been back home for a long time. No wonder everything seemed much smaller and more cramped than his childhood memories allowed.

So now Louis Kissinger read out his prepared speech. When his son Henry looked back on that moment thirty years later, he said his father had delivered the better speech, the true one that day. The old man, who had publicly returned almost four decades after his exile, spoke in German when he said that the city had 'always been close to his heart': 'I wasn't born in Fürth, but I

Louis Kissinger
615 Fort Washington Avenue
New York, New York 10040

Rede anläßlich der Verleihung der "Goldenen
Bürgermedaille" an Dr. Henry A. Kissinger

Fürth, Dezember 15, 1975.

Sehr verehrter Herr Bundesaussenminister,
sehr verehrter Herr Oberbürgermeister
sehr geehrte Festgäste,

Ich möchte zunächst meinen und
meiner Frau herzlichen Dank aussprechen
für die Einladung zu dem Ehrentag
unseres Sohnes. Ich betrachte es als eine
besondere Auszeichnung an dieser Feier
teilnehmen zu können, nicht nur weil
die Verleihung der Goldenen Bürgermedaille
eine grosse Anerkennung unseres Sohnes
bedeutet, sondern weil diese Ehrung
von einer Stadt erfolgt, die immer
meinem Herzen nahe stand. Zu meiner grossen Wertschätzung der Stadt
Fürth trug vor allem mein Studium
der Geschichte der Stadt vor mehr als

Coming home: Louis Kissinger means what he says. Manuscript of his speech on the presentation of the Citizen's Gold Medal to his son Henry, 15 December 1975.

spent most of my life in Germany in Fürth. It was here that I founded my family, here that my two sons were born, here that I spent the happiest years of my working life.'

And then Louis Kissinger spoke about Henry, said that it made him and his wife happy that their son had 'contributed to the international renown of the city of Fürth', said how proud they both were of their son, and used a phrase of his wife's: 'We are proud in humility! ... For us, his parents, it is a satisfying feeling to know that the word Kissinger is today synonymous with the word peace.' No one who heard the old man speak that day had any doubt that he meant what he said in his firm voice.

The occasion was also a family reunion, which happened in Fürth on that one and only time in thirty-seven years, when the four went together to the city's Jewish cemetery. Falk Stern, Paula's father, the grandfather of Heinz and Walter, was buried there. The public were excluded from the visit. Ambassador von Staden, who had a close relationship with the Kissingers and was therefore allowed to observe the scene from a distance, sensed how moved they all were during that moment of silent reflection. There are moments when one's whole life passes before one's eyes. That was such a moment, for all four of them.

After that, the family spent a little time together in the Park Hotel, where the parents were staying, and then the famous son had to get back to Nuremberg airport to be in Paris on time. Louis and Paula Kissinger stayed in the city and the surrounding area.

The next day became a journey through their early, happy life. They hadn't expected that a red carpet would be waiting for them in Leutershausen because they were actually going there for a 'private visit', as Louis said, touched and surprised by the official reception. Obviously, the old couple went to see Lore and Erika, the daughters of Karl and Babby Hezner, the only people who hadn't turned away from them after the Nazis came to power, but had always stood by them. And equally obviously, no cameras were present.

In the evening, the teacher, who had been forced into compulsory retirement in 1933, and who continued to receive his pension, graded according to income stage A 13, and whose doctors' bills were paid by the city of Fürth, met some of his former girl pupils. It was probably because of the abrupt end of his teaching career that they all felt as if the clock had stood still. 'Kissus could even still remember where his pupils had sat,' one of them said afterwards. And he later wrote to a teacher in Nuremberg who held on to the letter after the end of 1975: 'The affection of my former pupils, who are now old enough to be grandfathers and grandmothers, left me deeply moved.'

The last day belonged once more to Fürth. Although this wasn't on the official schedule, after the obligatory entry in the Golden Book they paid a visit to the Jewish religious community on Blumenstrasse. The two of them stood in silence in front of the panel of names of those who had not survived the campaign of persecution and extermination against the Jews of Fürth. There they found the name of Hugo Oppenheimer, at whose home Louis had lodged as a bachelor before he met Paula, the love of his life.

Louis and Paula Kissinger stopped on Julienstrasse to visit the synagogue before moving on to Tannenstrasse; Louis Kissinger, who had always practised the teaching profession with passion, wanted to pay a visit to his old workplace. He had taught for almost fifteen years at the Girls' Lyzeum, now the Helene-Lange-Gymnasium.

And that was enough. In every homecoming there is a risk, a danger of reopening old wounds. Certainly, Louis and Paula had long since found a new home in America, and when two days before, up in the bank canteen, Louis had looked down on his old city and on his life, he had no doubt that he 'had a debt of eternal gratitude to that great country, America' for opening up 'a fresh possibility of life' for him and his family. But he also said that they 'had to endure difficult years' there, because they had to construct a new life in a completely alien world, and because Louis Kissinger never really got over the fact that he couldn't practise his beloved profession any more.

Now that he was back in the city that was 'always close to his heart', it all came flooding back. After all those years, the meetings and memories of those days were beautiful and moving, but they were mingled with melancholy and grief. On the morning of 18 December 1975 Louis and Paula headed back to America. They would never see Fürth again.

Not so their sons, who were at the peak of their careers. That was true for Henry, and it was also true for Walter. In 1969, when the elder of the two marked the last stage of his meteoric rise with his appointment as Nixon's security adviser, his brother was thinking of saying goodbye to his professional career. Now in his mid-forties, the fact that he had enough money to keep himself and all six members of his family testified to a better than average career, and also to a considerable level of ambition. However they might have differed in other respects, that was one quality that the two brothers shared; and, of course, one has to wonder, would they have been able to develop and display that quality under different circumstances of life?

At any rate, because a return to a career in the diplomatic service, on which he had briefly embarked, was now out of the question, and because early retirement wasn't fulfilling, and strenuous and time-consuming sports like horse-riding did not use up all his energy, in 1969 Walter accepted an offer from the Allen Group, became a member of the board, and over the next few years reached the peak of his professional career.

The Allen Group, an internationally established producer of,

The younger, richer Kissinger: The American magazine Fortune *on Walter Kissinger, 1982.*

among other things, car parts, motor assembly equipment, and mobile communications systems, was going through a difficult time. Because his job got off to a good start, and because his reputation as a successful redeveloper of weak companies preceded him, Walter was soon put forward to be president of the firm. He was not basically disinclined, but he did set conditions that he himself thought would be unacceptable, like moving the company headquarters from Chicago to New York, or, more precisely, close to his residence on Long Island.

It tells us as much about the desperate situation of the company as it does about the enormous reputation of its new president, that the firm complied with all his conditions. From now on, as president of the Allen Group, Walter Kissinger was in the immediate proximity of the stables where he kept his five white Arab horses. Being able to ride became a precondition, never expressly formulated, for a leading position in the company, because the president liked to pursue his business duties in the saddle.

This craze of his had no effect on his management style. Walter Kissinger was a consistent and hard-headed redeveloper. That was felt not least by the senior personnel whom the new boss held responsible for the desolate state of the company. Within five years these people had bought no fewer than twenty-five companies, most of which were in the red. As soon as he was in the saddle, Walter not only got rid of most of these, he fired almost the whole of the management team. In the mid-seventies, 95 per cent of the senior workforce had been appointed by Walter.

His redevelopment of the company worked. By the time he left the firm in 1988, after almost twenty years as president, he had built up and transformed the Allen Group into a modern technological firm, introducing it, among other things, to mobile phone technology, which was revolutionary at the time. The company opened branches in western Europe and Japan, and became one of the pioneers in the huge new market that opened up in the wake of his brother Henry's diplomatic offensive in the People's Republic of China.

In one other respect too, Walter Kissinger was among the pioneers of modern American business history, one of its avant-garde thinkers. The seventies and eighties were a time of corporate takeovers: financially powerful companies bought up firms to break them down and sell their component parts, bringing in profits, but often at the expense of the workforce. Walter was a resolute opponent of such deals, for business reasons and also, if one may say so, on ethical grounds. Hollywood, which devoted a number of films to the subject, gave this type of converted businessman a popular face in the form of Richard Gere in *Pretty Woman*.

Walter Kissinger went public with his intentions, writing, for example, the *New York Times*, warning about such actions. 'Our values', he wrote in 1983 for *the Science Publishing Society*, 'have changed so dramatically that the attack may be seen as a fixed component of the strategy of serious enterprises. The quickly increasing trend towards forced takeovers is creating a hostile business atmosphere.' Certainly, there were winners. But it was far easier, Walter Kissinger said, 'to list the losses, because in terms of people, productivity and confidence there are many'.

Those were not empty words. Former colleagues from the upper strata of the Allen Group, such as Stephen Gilhuley or Don Bindler, speak with admiration even today of Walter's convictions and his management style. Certainly, he asked a 'whole lot' of his staff, and had a 'very intense' management style; but he was also a visionary, a very good negotiator and, above all, an unusually loyal boss. 'Walter Kissinger', says Don Bindler, 'is extraordinarily loyal to his friends, but also to the people around him – both inside and outside the company.'

Such public statements don't mean that the manager sought publicity; unlike his brother Henry, Walter 'dreaded the spot-

A shoulder to lean on: Walter and Genie Kissinger aboard the Queen Elizabeth II *in the Atlantic, mid-1970s.*

light', as *Newsweek* wrote in the mid-seventies. In that regard, the characterization of the captain of industry as 'The Other Kissinger' is entirely accurate. He was the other one, but he was still a Kissinger, and Walter, as he said in old age, had always known that the name Kissinger was 'not a disadvantage'.

But he never exploited it. Walter Kissinger was proud to have gone his own way, and to have enjoyed great success without the help of his brother. For example, on his many trips abroad he was always careful not to require the help of an American embassy. And he didn't need the preferential treatment that would have been almost inevitable in such a case. Strictly speaking, Walter was already a made man when his elder brother was striving for his professional career. Small wonder that Walter and Genie brought up their children to forge careers for themselves without reference to their family name.

That was important even after Henry left the State Department, because his voice and his name still carried weight, and he knew how to market the one with the help of the other. After the Democrat Jimmy Carter won the presidential elections in 1976 – a tight race, but a victory nonetheless – it was clear that Henry Kissinger's political career was coming to an end, after eight years. Privately, he and Nancy moved to the East Side of Manhattan and had a country retreat not far from Kent in Connecticut. Professionally, Henry began a new and no less successful career in Washington and New York.

He did not seriously consider returning to his teaching post at Harvard, which had been kept open for him throughout all those years. More interesting were three other paths that lay ahead of him. First, he was in great demand as a gifted after-dinner speaker. Then he signed a series of lucrative contracts as adviser to banks and companies, starting with Goldman, Sachs & Co. Finally, media concerns like NBC and the *Los*

Angeles Times took him on as a commentator and adviser.

After it had become clear that Henry Kissinger had no prospect of becoming Secretary of State in Ronald Reagan's government, and a third volume of his memoirs was not currently under discussion, from 1982 he concentrated entirely on his company. Shortly after he left office, Kissinger Associates, a unique kind of company, had been founded. Admittedly its titular head had a whole series of renowned partners, including Brent Scowcroft and Lawrence Eagleburger. But in fact it was a company designed to market the Kissinger name. That it flourished both massively and in the long term says much about the enormous reputation that he had accumulated over three decades.

But there was a price to pay for all this. The great effort involved, and also the unhealthy lifestyle, left their traces: Kissinger was seriously overweight, for example. In 1982, at just under sixty, he had a major bypass operation. That year became one of the most difficult of his adult life. As soon as he had recovered from the operation, his father died. At ninety-five, Louis Kissinger had reached the age of Solomon, and that had enabled him to follow and to enjoy the advancement and the great careers of both his sons.

Of course, he had never forgotten the things inflicted on him in Germany. How he suffered from the loss of his beloved teaching profession! And into great old age he repeatedly reminded people how difficult the early days in America had been. But in precisely that same context, Louis Kissinger always openly expressed his pride at the extraordinary success of his sons. Collecting, arranging, filing and commenting upon newspaper articles about them and their careers remained one of his favourite activities until the last. And it would certainly have given him great satisfaction to know of the honours that still awaited the elder of the two, in particular – not least in Germany, in Franconia.

Henry Kissinger had not been there since he had been awarded the Citizen's Gold Medal. Thirteen years passed before he came back to his home town, but then the intervals became shorter – because particular invitations and obligations required as much, or because the urge to revisit Fürth intensified with age. He was here again in 1988. In the year when his brother Walter finally retired from the management of the Allen Group in order to concentrate on voluntary activities, Henry was offered a further honour, this time by Fürth's neighbouring city of Erlangen, or, more precisely, its university.

On 19 March 1988 Henry Kissinger was awarded an honorary doctorate by the Friedrich Alexander University of Erlangen-Nuremberg. This brought him back to his old home town for the first time in thirteen years. Unlike the time when he was awarded the Citizen's Gold Medal of the city of Fürth, this time some critical voices were raised. They pointed out that Henry Kissinger's time in office as Secretary of State had coincided with the American war in Vietnam and Cambodia, as well as controversial American activities in South America, surrounding the overthrow of the Chilean president Salvador Allende, for example.

In Erlangen the Green Party, the peace movement, and large numbers of students announced their protest under the slogan 'Henry's coming – so are we'. A coalition of Greens, communists and peace activists distributed flyers saying, 'Henry Kissinger isn't welcome here'; and a Fürth city councillor who wanted to find out the cost of the, as always, sumptuous reception paid for by Kissinger's home town was brusquely, unanimously and formally forbidden to discuss the matter by his own faction on the council, the Socialist Party.

Weeks before the event, Fürth's officials were rushing around like mad, particularly since this time their guest had even planned to come for twenty-four hours: for the visit to his home town, for the formal awarding of the honour, and for a visit to Nuremberg's Franconia Stadium. When he arrived in Nuremberg on 18 March, the first thing on his schedule was an hour-long discussion with defence minister Manfred Wörner, who had flown in specially from Bonn, as had the American ambassador, Richard Burt. Henry Kissinger certainly knew how to hold court.

In Fürth there was the usual programme: press conference, Golden Book, ceremonial banquet, with, among others, the honorary citizens 'Doctor' Max Grundig and 'Professor' Grete Schickedanz, and a tour of the city. This time it was a nocturnal whistle-stop tour, and so that the city's guest could see everything, the fire brigade floodlit the house where he was born and the house where he had later lived, on Mathildenstrasse and Marienstrasse.

The award was made in the castle of Erlangen University at 10 o'clock the next day. As early as June 1986 a group of university lecturers in the two philosophy faculties of the Friedrich Alexander University had requested that Henry Kissinger be awarded the degree of honorary doctor of philosophy. The reason given was his extensive academic work, along with an assumption: 'At the FAU Kissinger – had he not been forced to emigrate to the USA by political developments in Germany – would in all probability have begun his academic training, and here he would presumably have begun a successful university career.'

The committees responsible quickly agreed, but unfortunately there was no free space in Henry's diary. It couldn't happen until just under two years later, when Henry Kissinger was able to receive his certificate in the castle of the university. Five hundred protestors were assembled outside, held in check by 250 police; inside, an educationalist acting as dean and a political scientist acting as official speaker established a happy medium. By now, in fact, even some of those who had made the original application were keeping their distance.

And what about the honorary doctor himself? As always, he held his cards close to his chest and at first, as the diarist of the local paper had it, made the usual 'slightly awkward joke about his modest command of German', then reflected, in English and in his usual superior manner, upon the problems of global politics. Only at one point did he become personal, and there was a sense that he meant what he said: 'I regret that my father cannot be here.' Still, Louis Kissinger had studied there after the First World War. And who could doubt that it would have filled Kissinger's father, the passionate teacher who had been forcibly retired, with joy, pride and probably not a little satisfaction, had be been there when that same university awarded his son an honorary doctorate?

Kissinger remained in the university town for less than five hours, before leaving – with a police escort, it goes without saying – for the third and last part of his programme. With the mayors of Erlangen, Fürth and Nuremberg, and the American ambassador in his wake, Henry Kissinger was driven to the Nuremberg Stadium. There he satisfied a long-nurtured desire and, for the first time in his life, saw a German football league match – not his own club, Spielvereinigung Fürth, which was at the time a long way from the German first division, but 1. FC Nürnberg, who on this occasion beat FC Homburg, who were bottom of the league, with a score of two-nil.

Like all personalities with similar biographies, Henry Kissinger had been working on his image in history for a long time. That is quite understandable, since, for all his distinctions, merits and successes, there was a problematic, or at least disputed, chapter in the politician's life. For that reason – and because he hadn't exactly disappeared from the scene even after leaving the State Department, but instead had remained a huge public presence at home and abroad – following his time in office legions of journalists, political scientists and historians had been working to dismantle his image.

There were ways of combating this, including the writing of his own memoirs, a project he had embarked upon after the end of his time in political office. In 1979 and 1982 he published two fat volumes, each of about three thousand closely printed pages, but even then they did not go beyond 1974. In 1994 he complemented these with a volume about the nature of foreign policy, which can also be read as a way of positioning the role of Henry Kissinger in recent history.

In late February 1994 an ABC television crew turned up in Fürth. Barbara Walters, the first lady of American television and a close friend of Henry Kissinger, wanted to make a film about his life for the legendary series *20/20*, and to film on location with him. Since the news had arrived at Fürth city hall only four weeks previously, there was a sense of emergency, particularly since the mayor planned to be in Kenya, for non-work-related reasons, on the date in question. There was no question, there had to be an official reception.

And the reception did take place, although it was all organized rather hastily because the important guest, tanned and good-humoured, arrived two hours later than expected. Meanwhile, the city officials and a number of policemen were kept waiting, along with the only invited guest. Werner Gundelfinger, a childhood friend, had been in the parallel class to Henry's at the Jüdische Realschule, and had played football with him on the Israelitische Turn- and Sportverein's playing field – until he and his brothers had left the city, two years before Henry and Walter.

Of course, they talked about the Nazi period. When Henry said it was time to 'draw a line under that period', German observers of the scene became irritated – as if Henry had meant drawing a final line. He had meant moving on, and that had nothing to do with forgetting, quite the contrary. After the end of filming he visited his grandfather's grave again, this time on his own.

By now the rest was routine. Henry Kissinger, who was chairman of the United States Organizing Committee for the hosting of the World Cup in the USA, accepted the invitation to see a match by his home team against Bayreuth, although Spielvereinigung Fürth was still playing in the Bavarian League; and he also attended the dinner to which the city invited the bearer of the Citizen's Gold Medal. It was still his city – or it had become his city once again. That was how Fürth saw it, because for a long time it had recognized what he meant for the city.

On 17 December 1997 Fürth city council decided, unanimously, and on the recommendation of the council of elders, to award Henry Kissinger honorary citizenship on the occasion of his seventy-fifth birthday. Until then, Fürth had been rather economical with that honour. Only three people since the Second World War had received the award, and all three were entrepreneurs: Gustav Schickedanz in 1958, Max Grundig in 1963, and Grete Schickedanz, who had continued the family business after her husband's death, in 1981. No politician had been granted the honour since 1945, not even Ludwig Erhard, perhaps Fürth's most famous son. The city council had not been able to force that one through at the time, since it was not altogether clear how he had benefited his home town.

So now it was Henry Kissinger's turn. Not only did he accept the invitation, he was even able to be in Fürth on Wednesday, 20 May 1998, the suggested date. Now it was a question of sorting out the schedule, because unfortunately Dr Kissinger could only spare a few hours. They were familiar with that problem by now. On the schedule, before the actual ceremony, was a visit to Spielvereinigung Fürth in the Ronhof. After the award in the Stadthalle came a brief press conference, lunch in the Kartoffel and, without the press, a visit to the Jewish cemetery. As on previous occasions, Henry Kissinger wanted to visit his grandfather's grave.

Anyone of any importance was invited: members of the Bavarian Cabinet, secretaries of state, members of parliament, district administrators, advisers, mayors, city councillors, Chancellor Helmut Kohl and foreign minister Klaus Kinkel, the party chairmen from the German Bundestag, as well as former Chancellor Helmut Schmidt, former president Walter Scheel, and the man who was foreign minister for many years, Hans-Dietrich Genscher. Others, invited at the express wish of Henry Kissinger, were the editors of *Der Spiegel* and *Die Zeit*, Rudolf Augstein and Marion Countess von Dönhoff, and 'Mrs Louis Kissinger', meaning Henry's mother Paula, as well as Ernst O. Krakenberger, believed to be Henry's only relative still living in the area.

Most of them declined for reasons of health or other commitments, including Marion Dönhoff (although she did send a written portrait of Henry Kissinger to Fürth), Rudolf Augstein, and the Chancellor. He was represented by his foreign minister and also sent a message in which he expressly thanked Henry Kissinger 'for always staying connected to your old homeland, which you were forced to leave during the time of the unjust National Socialist regime'.

Among those who did make it to Fürth were Hans-Dietrich Genscher and Helmut Schmidt. They both knew what Germany owed to this man. Even today, they have no doubt about it: 'He did a great deal to help Germany on its way to the community of democratic states,' says Genscher, 'and I think that the sympathy for Germany and Europe that he helped to create in America did much to bring about a situation whereby the Americans stood quite unambiguously and unreservedly behind German

*Honorary citizen: award of the honorary citizenship of Fürth to
Professor Dr Henry Kissinger by Mayor Wilhelm Wenning,
20 May 1998.*

efforts to achieve a unified state.' Schmidt also thought Germany owed a debt of gratitude to this man, 'for doing so much to ensure that many leading politicians in other countries understood the honesty of German efforts after 1945 and after 1948'.

Small wonder, then, that Henry Kissinger was pleased by both men's participation in the Fürth ceremony, and particularly by the fact that Helmut Schmidt was willing to speak in his honour. By his own account, the former Chancellor 'had been friends with this man for four decades'. Henry listened patiently as Helmut Schmidt put the audience in the picture about what he saw as the miserable state of the world – not a trace of personal memories.

Unlike Henry, who, in so far as it was possible in the context, once again expressed his closeness to the city and the country, and pointed out that he had already said as much when he had had to leave sixty years previously: '... when we were packing in Marienstrasse, a customs man came in and I said to him, "One day I'll come back here."' Since then he had returned to the city several times, but he still saw that day as the 'completion, the culmination' – at least that was what he said, and left it at that.

There were no reproaches and no accusations, just a sad memory of what the city and the country meant to the family, and what they had lost in 1938. Henry Kissinger didn't even put that in his own words, he referred instead to what his parents had said. The fact that on this occasion, in this place, he quoted verbatim the words that his father had uttered twenty-five years previously, when his son was awarded the Citizen's Gold Medal, tells us much – about him, his parents, and their relationship with each other. Then, when he read out a letter that his mother had given him to bring with him, one could once again have heard a pin drop: 'I share', wrote the old lady, who was no longer capable of travelling, 'in my thoughts, in pride and in humility, this celebration.'

Beyond the grave: Walter Kissinger with his children Dana and John by the graveside of Karl and Babby Hezner in Leutershausen, August 1981.

Humility – that was the fundamental attitude of this extra-ordinary woman towards a most unusual life. Six months later, on 15 November 1998, Paula Kissinger died, at the age of ninety-eight. In mid-December her son Henry thanked the city of Fürth for its expression of sympathy on the part of its citizens, and confirmed once again: 'My mother always had a warm spot in her heart for Fürth, regardless of the difficult years.' She left her two sons Henry and Walter, six grandchildren, and six great-grandchildren.

Until her death, Paula Kissinger lived in the apartment at 615 Fort Washington Avenue which the family had moved into in 1940. Even the furniture was essentially the inventory that had reached the Kissingers months after their expulsion from Germany. Walter and Genie – who looked after her mother-in-law until the last, and wore her wedding-ring after her death – tried to persuade Paula to move, but without success. Henry, too, repeatedly tried to persuade his mother to move in with him and Nancy in their spacious apartment on the Upper East Side, but again in vain. A weekend in their country house or a holiday with Walter and Genie in Puerto Rico – all fine and good. But she didn't want to move house.

Not even after a severe accident: one day she fell in the kitchen, lay there unconscious, and was only found by neigh-bours several hours later. When the doctors advised Henry to avoid any life-prolonging measures, as his mother would never be able to think or speak clearly again, he said: 'You don't know my mother.' When she awoke from her coma days later, she asked her son, who was keeping watch by her sick-bed, 'What day is it today?' When Henry replied, 'Tuesday,' she asked him to cancel her dentist's appointment. Paula Kissinger herself told this story a few years before her death. You can see how the family survived the difficult years in Fürth.

So the old lady went on living in the apartment that she had lived in for over half a century, went to Fort Tryon Park, weather permitting, took out a cushion, and sat down on a bench – whenever possible the same one, the one she had sat on with Louis. After Paula's death her sons fixed memorial plates to both that and the neighbouring bench, each with a line of poetry. Henry and Walter commemorated Paula with the words of Thomas Bailey Aldrich: 'What is lovely never dies, but passes into other loveliness'. And how could the essence of Louis Kissinger have been more appropriately grasped in words than with a phrase by Johann Wolfgang von Goethe, from his conversations with Eckermann: 'Alles Edle ist an sich stiller Nature' – 'Everything noble is essentially silent by nature.'

Sometimes when Paula sat here towards the end of her life, one of the other survivors of the 'Fourth Reich' would come by. Then these old people would exchange a word – mostly in English, sometimes in German: 'Only when we talk about the war,' she said in 1997, 'we always speak German.' So the country of her early years became the pivot and fulcrum in the thoughts and feelings of Paula Kissinger, née Stern, until her death, for both good and ill.

The same wasn't true of her sons Henry and Walter. Certainly, they came to Germany from time to time – Henry more than Walter, not least because his work often took him there. But unlike their parents, they had no profound, lifelong connection. At least Walter didn't.

Henry never came to Fürth on the spur of the moment. There had to be a reason, whether it was for an award, an engagement as a public speaker, or to participate in a conference. And when he was in the area, he never stayed longer than was absolutely necessary, at least after the 1950s. After that he never went to Leutershausen either, and one has the impression that his avoidance of the place had nothing to do with the pressure of his diary. As he grew older, Henry clearly found it harder to go back to the place where Heinz had probably spent the happiest years of his life.

Not so Walter. He was emotionally robust – no less sensitive than his brother, but hardier in this respect. He had finished with that chapter of his life early on, and was quite consistent about it. Not only could he live in a kind of German milieu, in a house on Long Island that from the outside looked almost like a miniature German castle, drive German motorbikes and cars, and always keep a German shepherd dog, with a German name. It was also easy for him to return to the places of his childhood, at least easier than it was for Henry, for whom it was a very emotional matter – so much so that he avoided some places entirely and in his professional life ticked off others as quickly as possible, treating them as stops in a very busy schedule.

Of course, such visits were harder for Henry than they were for his brother, because Walter's visits to Fürth and Leutershausen didn't exactly attract hordes of journalists. Thus Walter was able to plan his trips and appear in the city more casually. He wanted to maintain the connection with his first home, and he also wanted to bring it closer to his children; consequently the four of them not only learned German at school, albeit with different levels of success, but they all visited Fürth and Leutershausen at least once.

In the fifties, sixties and seventies, Walter himself used journeys to Europe to make side-trips to Franconia. At the end of 1981 he went there with his youngest son John and his daughter Dana, who would later live in Switzerland and travel to Leutershausen with her husband. Tom Kissinger, who of all Walter's children engaged most intensely with the history of the family, and who visited his old grandmother in New York almost every week until she died, went there with a group of young people in June 1986. He spent three days looking around his father's and

Grandpa we love you: Walter Kissinger with his daughter Dana (left) and his granddaughters.

grandparents' home, and he was entertained by the Hezners' daughters. Two and a half years later, in December 1988, Walter's eldest son was also drawn to visit the family's old home: on the way from Vienna to see his sister in Geneva, Bill Kissinger stopped off in Leutershausen.

This was not true of Henry, or of his children. He hadn't been seen in Leutershausen since the fifties, and he only came to Fürth when there was a reason, as in 1995, when the Schickedanz family engaged him as an after-dinner speaker on the occasion of the hundredth birthday of the founder of the Quelle mail-order company.

Things were not dissimilar now, in June 2004. An event in Bamberg was the reason for the eighty-one-year-old political star to stop off in Franconia on the way from Italy to China. And because his brother Walter was soon to celebrate his eightieth birthday, the elder brother invited the younger to come along. So the brothers' trip to the city of their childhood and youth became a 'sentimental journey', a melancholy voyage into the past.

That reveals the good relationship between Henry and Walter Kissinger; and there were reasons for this, above all the fact that the younger brother had stepped aside to let his elder brother shine. Luckily, Walter himself never needed public appearances, in fact he dreaded them. Even in the seventies, when both men were at the peaks of their careers – the elder as security adviser and foreign envoy, the younger as president of an industrial concern – Walter never tried to steal the show from Henry.

Even if we take into account the fact that he could hardly have managed to do so, because the media was treating Henry like a Hollywood star at the time, this reticence is remarkable because it reveals something about the character of the man.

Walter Kissinger, who was already set up for life by his mid-forties, was self-contained. The confirmation that his brother Henry – himself, through his own profession, a made man in his mid-forties – sought in public appearances, the younger brother found in his job, increasingly in sport, above all horse-riding, and, of course, in his family.

The older Walter became, the more voluntary positions he held. At the centre of his many activities were conservation and social or charitable work. Of particular importance to him was the family foundation, which he ran with his wife Genie, and in which his children were also involved. 'Twice a year', Genie reports, 'the family meets up in various places to talk about the previous year's activities, and to discuss which individuals or institutions we should support and sponsor in future. Walter and Tom ensure that it is run accordingly.'

Walter's involvement with school projects in Cambodia, among other things, has a certain piquancy. Admittedly it wasn't his idea; it was Bernhard Krisher, the foreign correspondent of *Newsweek* and a friend of Walter's, who persuaded him to take an interest. But who can think of Cambodia without remembering the invasion of that South-East Asian country by American troops, and thus of the man in charge of American foreign policy in 1970?

Seeing the two old men walking through their German home town today is very moving – because one knows their early history, and because old people, like children, prompt protective impulses. One should not be deceived. Both were and are to some extent still resolute, energetic, ambitious men: one at the lectern, the other in the saddle. And if people like these two had, in their mid-forties, achieved more or less everything that could realistically be achieved, they must have had a considerable amount of ambition, and, when it came to it, they couldn't have been shy about using their elbows to get where they wanted to be.

In this respect the two men are very similar, for all their other differences. That should not come as a surprise, because they weren't just brothers: as children and adolescents they also shared a single fate. What career paths they might have followed under other circumstances, what successes they might have enjoyed in Germany, we cannot tell. But it is quite plain that their American careers would have been unthinkable if they hadn't been forced to start all over again.

That gives their return to their old home a special touch. The appearance of the two men in Fürth revealed both what they shared and what distinguished them. Just as Henry, by his own declaration, allowed his brother to step into the foreground in the television documentary where the family was concerned, Walter let his brother take the stage when they appeared together. No question about who was the dominant one here, and no question, either, that Walter had no problem with that distribution of roles.

For the city, of course, the visit was an event, as always. Thus, apart from the obligatory entry in the Golden Book, a lunch in the Kartoffel followed by a press conference were on the official part of the programme. The unofficial part involved the places of their childhood, above all the football stadium in Ronhof, now known as the Playmobil Stadium, where Greuther Fürth, as the Spielvereinigung is now called, has its home. Then they passed their parents' house on the way to their grandfather's grave in the Jewish cemetery.

From Bamberg, where they were staying, both men were to have paid a visit to the Hezners' daughters in Leutershausen. But then Henry had to attend to his brother, who had fallen ill, before setting off to Washington to take part in the funeral ceremony for President Ronald Reagan. Again, one has the impression that the occasion was timely. A visit to Leutershausen, a brief detour on the way to the airport, would hardly have raised serious problems where his schedule was concerned. Flights to Washington leave at hourly intervals.

Walter had to pull out of the visit as well, because he had to go to hospital. Luckily it wasn't the stroke that some had feared. Exhaustion, an untreated infection, jet lag, and the powerful emotional experience had laid Walter low; after all, he was nearly eighty now. The doctors of the St Getreu Bamberg hospital dealt with the emergency; and Henry, who was already on the way to America, later thanked the city for saving his brother in a few lines accompanied with a cheque. That Walter did the same was obviously not considered headline-worthy.

Walter already felt better the following day, so he at least was able to go to Leutershausen. This time his wife Genie went along as well. In fact, her visit hadn't been planned, but when she learned of her husband's collapse she had got on the next plane and travelled to Bamberg. So it was that on 12 June 2004 Walter's wife also went to Leutershausen, for the second time in her life.

It was four years earlier, almost to the day, that Genie Kissinger had last visited the Hezners' daughters, as a detour on a trip to Europe. Certainly she was interested in Walter's family history because Walter was her husband, but as he had dealt with that story a long time ago and it was not an issue, or not an immediately burdensome one, Genie had never felt any strong desire to trace her husband's roots.

The brothers' trip to Fürth, their 'sentimental journey', in June 2004, was something special because, apart from the family reunion in 1975, it was their first and only trip together to their home town since they had been forced to leave almost sixty years before. They didn't give much away about themselves in Fürth. Why should they? They knew what had brought them there. If the city had been indifferent to him, as someone suggested to Henry, he certainly wouldn't have gone there.

And he announced quite explicitly, also speaking on behalf of his brother, that if everything goes well, if they remain in good health, they will be back – in the autumn of 2007 at the latest, when Fürth celebrates its jubilee year. And then, if not before, they will see me again, the one who wrote down their story and, by doing so, found them.

How I found Henry and Walter

When the brothers leave Fürth on that remarkable 7 June 2004, I am in cheerful spirits. Henry had agreed: 'I'll give you the interview. But not now and not here in Fürth. Unfortunately you'll have to come to America, but I will give you the interview!' Those were his words. I want to go to America anyway, and I had to, to film in the places where the Kissingers lived after their escape from Germany. And I want to do the interview with Walter.

When the date has been agreed for the visit to Walter's ranch in Colorado, I call Henry's New York office. Perhaps I'll be lucky. Perhaps he'll be in town. Perhaps I can kill several birds with one stone. Unfortunately nothing comes of it. 'Sadly Dr Kissinger isn't available in New York.' His schedule, I know ... Once again it's Jessica P. Incao, 'Jessee' for short, who puts me in the picture. Over the coming weeks and months she will become a crucial figure on the road to Henry, and that road will be longer and stonier than I assume in summer 2004.

On the other hand, my relationship with Walter and Genie is getting better and better. Since I visited their ranch at the end of August it's almost turned into a friendship. At any rate, Walter is willing to accompany me to some of the places that were significant in his early life in America: Washington Heights, the new home of the Kissinger family after their expulsion from Fürth; and Princeton, the first and most important stop in Walter's academic career.

But the closer the date gets, the higher the hurdles become on the way to Princeton and New York. First of all Gofer, Walter's favourite horse, falls ill, and that takes up all his attention. Then it turns out that Walter's sons Tom and John have no idea that their father has set up an interview with them for me. They are both planning to run in the New York marathon, take a shower, and then get back to New Jersey or California as soon as possible. And I can quite understand if they don't want to use the little time they have talking to an unknown journalist from Germany, but would rather have dinner with their parents.

But more than anything it becomes clear once again how difficult it is for Walter to make that journey into the past. Late in October, a few days before I leave for America, he phones and asks me to understand his reservations about my project: the years in Washington Heights weren't necessarily the happiest of his life. By now, however, I know Walter and I am sure: once I am there, he'll open up. And that's what happens.

On 3 November 2004 I am off back to America: Singapore Airlines from Frankfurt to New York. That's the nice bit of the journey. It gets difficult at the airport. First of all we have to go through all kinds of obstacles with our equipment at Kennedy Airport, because again I am travelling with a German camera crew. At last, when we have found our hire car, our navigation system starts creating considerable problems. But we do manage to get to Manhattan. On Walter's recommendation I've booked a room at the Waldorf Astoria, where there's already a message waiting for me: 'Welcome to America – Walter!' Well then!

The next morning I am up at five, which means I've got the whole day – and I need it, because I am on a very tight schedule, and there's no production company waiting in the background to sort everything out for me. I am a one-woman show: scriptwriter, director, producer, presenter, secretary, make-up artist – everything. That has its advantages, because it makes meetings in front of the camera more human, authentic, believable.

Apart from anything else, it means I can present myself in any way I like. And when I am filming, particularly with one of the two brothers, I feel good. Although the early starts, the long, strenuous filming days, the car journeys, the changeable weather, and all the conversations in a foreign language, drain the energy, you can't tell from looking at me. I feel happy and level-headed.

On the very first day we are filming at the Empire State Building, then in Washington Heights. For the first time I feel that I, too, have certain inhibitions about my project. I have to think about people and their fates. Could there be anyone else living here who was able to escape the campaign of persecution and extermination in thirties Germany? Perhaps even someone from Fürth or Nuremberg? I feel like an intruder, and avoid filming people or nameplates in close-up; and I can't summon the courage to ask anyone about Paula Kissinger, who lived here until her death six years ago. I furtively look at some house doorways. Sure enough, there they are – among the American and Spanish names, some German ones: Stern, Fein, Rosenberg ...

Back at the hotel, a beautiful bouquet and a phone message from Walter remind me that it's my birthday: 'Happy Birthday Evi!' A lovely way of getting into the right frame of mind for the following day, when I have meetings with Walter and Genie. In his office on Long Island I also finally get to meet Anne. She is Walter's Jessee, you might say.

The day itself is extraordinarily hectic, because it's full of shooting schedules, because Walter and Genie are elderly and unused to television cameras, because things keep getting in the way. For example, some photograph albums that haven't been mentioned before. Walter has had two identical copies made of an album – one for me, one for himself – in which the most important stages of his life are documented: everything painstakingly numbered and captioned in tiny writing. But above all, at his house in the evening, he shows me an album that Tom gave his mother Genie for her birthday: the story of 'Mama K.', as Paula is called in the family.

I am allowed to film everything, the early photographs from Germany, the school reports, the passports – absolutely everything. Fantastic! The shots in the office work, but Walter's schedule puts us under a lot of pressure; he has no idea of the pressure involved in our work. He wants to spend time with me, talk to me, go to dinner with me, show me his home. The camera is of secondary importance, a necessary evil.

The next day Princeton is on the agenda – a football game, a visit to Walter's club, then a glimpse of his former student room. But most importantly, Walter has his dissertation for his undergraduate degree fetched from the archive. It's been there for over fifty years, since he handed it in. He himself no longer owns a copy of his study of Russian policy in East Asia between 1895 and 1904. And it ends with a remarkable perspective on the period in which it was written, the early fifties. I shoot that passage for my film. When the two brothers look at it a year later, Henry asks in amazement, 'Did you write that?'

I can't yet guess any of that in November 2004. I have other worries. Unfortunately, Walter is always forgetting that I am here to film. The next day, for example, in the middle of New York City. Walter has come into the city in his cream-coloured Mercedes convertible. It gets a flat tyre, in Times Square of all places, the busiest spot in Manhattan. And as we stand there in the middle of the roaring traffic, he starts talking, about his early experiences, about Fürth, about Leutershausen. I urgently ask him not to tell me here and now. But he goes on, because the story has come into his head here and now, and he doesn't want to repeat things like that. Of course, the camera isn't ready. And time's marching on, because Walter wants to be at the finishing-line of the marathon in time to see his sons.

I am close to madness. But somehow with Walter things don't turn out as you expect them to. When I've given up any idea of success – by now we have reached Washington Heights – Walter forgets the camera, which is running this time, and starts talking – all in one piece, for almost an hour, as we walk through the park and Walter shows me the benches where his parents were so fond of sitting and which their sons later decorated with a line of poetry for each of them.

Then Walter takes me to Fort Washington Avenue and shows me the house where the family lived after their expulsion from Germany and an intermediate period in the Bronx on the other side of the river. He tells me where the apartment was. We don't go into the building. When I point to the names by the doorbells and ask him if there are any familiar names, he barely looks and just says, 'No, none.' And with that, Walter is back in the present; he politely says goodbye and leaves for the marathon with Genie. Later, my team and I do manage to film around the entrance to the building. Then, at the editing table, everything is skilfully put together and it looks as if I went with Walter into his first home on American soil and came back out with him.

On the Monday evening Walter invites me to a benefit concert in Carnegie Hall. I haven't got permission to shoot there, but Walter introduces me to a few people who might be important for my film. He does that, incidentally, as he did at the party in Colorado, with the observation: 'This is Evi. She is the Barbara Walters of Germany.' How embarrassing for me! Of course, I know that Barbara Walters is the *grande dame* of American television.

I get to meet some interesting people, above all Anita Helmrich and her husband Joe. He was born a German Jew in Cologne and, like the Kissinger family, managed to get out in 1938. She is an old and very good friend of the family; she knows a great deal about all four of them, and can talk about it in front of a camera. Anita Helmrich is a stroke of luck, and she is an attractive woman as well. When I am allowed to visit her in Westchester the following day, and she hands me copies of letters and notes from Paula and Louis Kissinger, I am very happy.

Nothing changes in that respect after I get back to Germany

on 11 November. At least not at first. But then reality catches up with me, and it has a name: Henry. Two phone calls to his office leave no doubt that nothing's going to happen this year. Jessee does what she can. At least, she says she does. But there's simply no room to be found in Henry's diary for that one hour. Walter, when I tell him, is very 'irritated' that his 'efforts over a whole year have been a failure', and adds: 'I am rather reluctant to open a fresh round.'

Was that it? Have I failed? Late in 2004 that's almost how it looks. Certainly, I've found Walter. And without a doubt that's a great blessing for which I am thankful and about which I am proud. It's more than I could have expected, and the experience has left me feeling strong. But for my film, in which I've already invested so much money and, more importantly, so many intense emotions, it's not enough. I need Henry. And I want to know. Didn't he promise me that interview back in June? I want him to keep his word. So I stay on the ball. Still. Now more than ever.

So I get to know Jessica P. Incao, because the way to Henry's office and thus to my interview leads through her. By now my phone calls to her have become a nightmare. Not because I find her unpleasant. I like her voice. But she doesn't just speak very quickly, Jessee always says what she has to say extremely succinctly, and what she has to say to me is generally bad news: one refusal after another.

In situations like that I find myself assailed by self-doubts that I am otherwise unfamiliar with. Have I taken on too much? Should I have left it at the short portrait that I'd originally planned for *Franconiaschau*, even if no one would have thought it was particularly interesting? And why should Henry K., who in his own words 'never gives interviews about his private life', have to answer questions from me, of all people?

And then I think about whether I really want to share what I've experienced, what I've been through, with the public, whether I even want to publish the film that I definitely want to make. And each time I come to the same conclusion: 'No, actually, I don't. What I'd really like to do is shut my eyes, lock everything away in my heart and keep it to myself.' But it's too late for that. Because my film is a promise to both of them, Henry included, that I will tell their story. And I have his assurance that he'll join in.

Today I get Jessee on the phone straightaway: Dr Kissinger is very busy, he hasn't got much time. Aha, I think, as usual. But then Jessee suggests taking a look in our diaries: what about April? Which week would suit? I can't believe my ears and just say, 'Any date is fine.' All right, then: Wednesday, 19 April, three o'clock in the afternoon? 'Of course, and where?' In his New York office. I am so speechless that I forget to ask her how much time I will have at my disposal. So when I call Jessee again she says Dr Kissinger has ten appointments a day and he'll give me twenty minutes. After twenty-one minutes at the most he will disappear. That's what he always does.

Can a person tell his life in twenty minutes? I am about to find out. There's no alternative. At any rate I make other appointments, with Marvin Kalb for example, one of Henry Kissinger's best biographers, and above all with Walter and Genie. By now the time fixed for my interview with Henry has already been moved, and on no account do I want to go home empty-handed. On 16 April I take my own crew back to New York, this time four men and two cameras.

First of all we use our stay to do some additional location shooting in Washington Heights: the synagogue, the college, the streets. Then, a day before the interview, we are briefly allowed into Henry's office to prepare for our filming. His office is on Park Avenue, diagonally opposite the Waldorf

Astoria, where I am staying again. I can see the imposing building from my window. There are no signs indicating who might be in there.

What does it look like inside? I find out the next day. After I leave the lift and pass a worn-out three-piece suite and a pane of glass with a young blonde woman sitting behind it, a massive wooden door opens, and, standing in the doorway, there she is. Jessee is quite different from what I had imagined: young, pleasant, rather mouse-like. We greet one another cordially; later I talk to her a little and next day I bring her a carefully selected bouquet, with which she is visibly delighted. She couldn't afford it herself, she says.

So today I am allowed to enter Henry's world. In fact, I am disappointed. The atmosphere is sobering: nothing special, certainly nothing statesmanlike. The whole thing is in urgent need of renovation, and it could certainly do with a lick of paint. There's lots of stuff lying around, even in the corridors: cardboard boxes, stacks of papers and newspapers, some bits of office furniture that no one needs any more. On the right there's an open office door, on the left Jessee's very small, very full office. At the end of the corridor on the right is Henry's office. Opposite it sits another very young woman, with a kind of counter in front of her covered with notes, sheets of paper, printed-out emails. On another occasion I see what's going on here: whenever he comes out of his office the first thing he does is look at this stack of papers.

The room set aside for the interview is terribly small and undistinguished. I recognize it from a few details. In October 2002 Henry gave Günter Gaus an interview here, for the *Zur Person* television programme. In 1962 Gaus had taken part in one of the famous summer schools that Kissinger organized at Harvard. His conversation with Henry was, like almost everything that the late Gaus did, good and informative. But Henry avoided referring to his early years.

191

I want to do it better. That involves, with Jessee's permission, rearranging the powder-blue-painted room for our interview tomorrow. So a few things, including a rubber plant, make their way into the corridor to contribute to the general chaos for a while. Staying inside, for the time being, are two massive wing chairs in which Henry and I will seat ourselves for the interview. It's a coincidence, of course, but Walter sat in just such a chair when I first met him in a London hotel in June 2003.

The next morning, Tuesday, 19 April 2005, I slip into my new apricot-coloured dress and make my way to Henry's office at about eleven o'clock. I am in a cheerful mood, I am looking forward to the interview, I am looking forward to Henry. When I get there Jessee tells me that it must on no account go over twenty minutes, and my boys, who have been setting up and doing the lighting for some time, tell me that Henry's clearly in a bad mood, that he snapped at them and referred to the twenty minutes. I am terribly disappointed to hear that. After all this time and all the obstacles I've had to overcome, I am close to tears, and what I'd really like to do is take the cameras down and go. No, not like that! No one treats me like that! Not even Henry Kissinger. I know I am not in the right mood to do a good interview with him.

But I am in his kingdom now, and when he briefly appears and gives me a very nice and charming greeting, my mood starts to improve, although he stresses once again: 'Regardless of what you ask, Frau Kurz, please, no more than twenty minutes.' A little while later he ushers me into his office for a preliminary chat. There are big picture frames with signed photographs, showing him with the world's prominent politicians, and also – almost slightly threatening, and hung slightly too high on the wall – a portrait of a blonde lady in pastel blues, whites and yellows: Nancy, his second wife. I don't imagine at the time that I'll ever get to meet her.

Henry asks me what I want to ask him about, and I say,

Two people from Fürth: New York, 19 April 2005.

'About your carefree childhood in Fürth, about your family and relations, and, of course, all the things that happened after the Nazis took power.' Henry nods, and as I've recovered myself I assure him once again that I am not trying to reveal anything hidden. I tell him about my research and the meetings and discussions with his brother, and express the hope that he can spare me a bit of time.

He actually looks at his watch and says he has to leave at one-thirty. If we hurry ... Then I give him the presents I've brought along, which I didn't want to give him initially because of the horrible atmosphere, as well as some carefully selected photographs of the caskets that I had had made for the two brothers, one each, based on an old Fürth coat of arms, made from a 150-year-old lump of beech wood. The tree once stood in Fürth city park. And a few leaves from the garden in Leutershausen, including one from a damson tree.

Henry is visibly moved, and if I am not very much mistaken I hear him say for the first and only time, in a slightly broken voice: 'From Grandfather's garden? From the garden in Leutershausen?' 'Yes, there's a very old damson tree there. That's the one I plucked the leaf from.' He clutches my forearm, presses it tightly, and says he hadn't expected that. That I'd taken so much trouble ... I sense that he really means it.

The interview is good and informative, not least because Henry states on camera that he never normally speaks about these things. More importantly, he gives me more than twenty minutes. Then, when I ask him for a photograph, he puts his arm around my waist, holds me nice and tightly, and asks me what I am going to tell his brother if he asks me how he behaved. Nicely? Or nastily? The question seems important to him. At any rate, he asks me the question again, puts his arm tightly around me again, and turns on all his charm. That way I end up with a series of lovely pictures – and he finally gets my answer. He likes it.

Walter likes it too. We have arranged to have dinner in the Princeton Club in Manhattan. Genie welcomes me, hugs me, takes me into her room, and tells me they have both been very tense and nervous all day. A little time later, Walter comes out of the library, beams at me, and hugs me as well. Then I tell them the whole story, from the beginning.

When I get to Henry's curt manners and tell him I came very close to getting up and leaving, Walter turns red in the face and tells me that his brother rang him up again three weeks ago and asked whether he, Walter, really wanted him, Henry, to give me, Evi, the interview. The rest of my account of my morning meeting with Henry then puts his mind at rest. Outside the club a photograph is taken of the three of us. Later Walter writes on it: 'For Evi – a great artist and a good friend.'

Over dinner we talk about this and that, including a very telling episode related by Walter. Some time after Nixon's resignation as president, Walter had invited Nixon to engage in discussions with a Chinese trade delegation, and said to him on that occasion: 'There's one thing you did very badly, and I am still aggrieved with you about it.' When Nixon, who had no sense of humour, froze, he explained to the ex-president: 'You appointed an unknown Harvard professor as Secretary of State, and in the process turned me into Henry Kissinger's brother.' More than two years after I began exploring the subject and met both men, I know what he means.

When I tell Walter over dinner that Henry repeatedly mentioned him in his answers he is very pleased, and Henry was clearly left with a good feeling as well. At least, a few days after I leave, Walter sums up the impression that the interview made on his brother in an email: 'He thinks you're an enchanting and very intelligent person, and seems to be very happy with the interview.'

Henry had indicated as much to me too, before I left New York. The morning after the interview, when I happen to run into

Henry, in a hurry as always, because I want to drop off a brief message for him in the lobby, he says he spoke to Walter the previous evening. They talked for a long time. But now he really has to go ...

So, incidentally, do I, because I've got an appointment with Marvin Kalb in Washington. We drive out of New York and meet in his office at eleven o'clock. Marvin Kalb is very tall, still good-looking, and very charming. It's a great interview. Kalb speaks precisely, winningly, and in much greater detail than I'd expected.

By the time my crew and I set off home to Germany I am exhausted. Emotionally and physically. Completely finished. Because of the meetings with the two brothers, the second with Henry, the fourth with Walter. And because of the chaos at the airport in Washington. Everything goes wrong. We walk in the wrong direction, stand in long queues at the wrong counters, can't find customs first of all and then don't have the right papers. Eventually, though, we are on the plane to New York, and once I get on the plane to Germany I sleep through absolutely everything – drinks, dinner, breakfast. I am woken up shortly before we land in Frankfurt. I am proud and happy, because the tapes of my interview with Henry are in my bag. Now I have the material for my film.

But I want more. Above all, I'd still love to have pictures and interviews with Walter's children, Henry's wife Nancy, and, if possible with Henry himself. He won't be available for an exclusive interview, that much is clear. But there may be an opportunity to observe him from close up. It happens sooner than I expect.

On 8 May 2005, Henry comes to Darmstadt and Heppenheim at the invitation of the prime minister of Hessen, Roland Koch, to take part in the commemorations for the sixtieth anniversary of the end of the war. Henry had mentioned it in New York, and said the date might be of interest to me – not just because it's an opportunity to see him again, but also because in Heppenheim he is going to be visiting the villa where he lived as a young officer with the American army of occupation. I need those pictures. And I get the opportunity – in the face of all opposition. In the end, I am the only one to get permission to film at Heppenheim – and an invitation to a very select dinner. All without recommendations or contacts.

But first, Darmstadt. Before Henry delivers his speech, there's a little reception by the prime minister with the members of his Cabinet. I manage to crash it. I don't know anyone, not one of the faces is familiar. That's clearly mutual. I am studied obliquely, but intensely: what's she doing here? But no one dares to speak to me.

Then they come: Koch at their head, gesticulating in a statesmanlike manner, Henry diagonally behind him, with a charming smile and his characteristic forward-hunching shoulders. I've taken up a position by the door. Henry, who has no idea that I am going to be there, sees me and tries to walk over in my direction, but the prime minister pushes him in the other direction. Protocol ... Once Henry has shaken hands with some minister or other, however, he turns round, comes beaming over to me and says, 'Oh, Evi, how lovely that you're here. I'm delighted to see you. Thank you for coming.' Evi! For the first time Henry calls me by my first name.

Koch ignores me and doesn't even say hello. Who cares? That's his problem. Once Henry has greeted everyone in the line, we go into the hall: Henry, Koch, the ministers, me in the middle. As Henry delivers his intelligent and informative speech, I have time to observe him. He doesn't look well, his face is pale yellow and puffy. He is doing too much. Walter has told me he has recently been in hospital – like Walter himself, both with heart conditions, both for the same operation. But

Henry has a history of this: heart attacks, bypasses and so on. I am worried about him.

Then Henry has finished. Applause, greetings, clusters of people. I stay in the background. When Henry spots me, he comes up to me once more, shakes my hand again, and says, 'Thank you, Evi, thank you for coming. I am really delighted. Thank you!' There isn't much time, not for the protocol, and not for my camera crew either. I've got two this time, one in Heppenheim and another ready and waiting in Darmstadt. Outside there are hundreds of onlookers, police on horseback, motorcycle escorts. Henry has barely taken his seat in the car when the procession starts moving.

I am in the middle of it all again, because I've been given permission to join the motorcade with my own car and driver. So we roar off, surrounded by flashing blue lights, all the way across Darmstadt, through red lights and blocked crossings, to the motorway. It's really quite exciting. You feel very important, and I understand why Henry doesn't want to stop being Henry.

The day ends with a generous dinner in Henry's former official villa. The twenty or so guests are mostly prominent faces from the worlds of German business and politics. I am seated on Henry's side, more or less at the other end of the table, so that I can't see him. During the general hubbub, when he threatens to leave without saying goodbye and I tap him gently on the shoulder from behind, he turns round and says, 'Oh, Evi, I was just looking out for you. A shame we didn't have the chance to talk undisturbed.' Of course, I don't give up, and suggest we meet for breakfast the following morning. But Henry declines. He has to go to China. 'See you.'

And I will see him again. Whenever. For the moment, I use my time for complementary shots and interviews, with Helmut Schmidt, for example, whom I've arranged to meet at the Hotel

Atlantik in Hamburg. It's a good, concentrated interview. It's actually the only time that the former Chancellor has ever spoken about Henry Kissinger like this. The two men have known and valued one another for years. But even Helmut Schmidt doesn't know that Henry Kissinger has a brother.

I am still in intense and very personal contact with him. Only once is there any kind of misunderstanding. When I ask Walter if he minds me talking to one or two of his old classmates, he gives me an unusually resolute refusal. For all the respect that he has for my devotion to journalism, neither he nor Henry wishes to revive relationships that lie more than sixty years in the past, regardless of whether they are used in the film or not.

On the other hand, Walter helps me to organize an appointment with his son Tom. This is a new dimension. For a long time I was refused access to Louis and Paula Kissinger's grandchildren. So now it's Tom, who I know was particularly close to his grandmother. He invites me to his house in New Jersey, not far from New York City. So, on 4 June 2005, I am back on the plane. It's my fourth trip to America for my film, and I have my own camera crew with me once again.

My expectations are limited, because Tom's enthusiasm has been limited in the run-up to our meeting. I have the feeling Tom is only doing this because of his parents. I am not staying in vibrant Manhattan, but in a glass palace somewhere in the green fields of New Jersey. But once again it doesn't happen as I'd imagined.

Next morning, when I show up at a pretty house on the edge of the forest and ring the doorbell at the agreed time, a man opens the door, tall, slim, boyish, not especially striking; visually at least, Tom isn't very like his father. But he has a close, deep relationship with both his parents. He is forty-three and has a family of his own: his wife Annette – slim, dark-blonde hair, confident, open, intelligent, modest – and two little daughters, one of whom is named after Tom's grandmother, Paula.

The third generation: 'Oma' Paula Kissinger with her grandson Tom, Walter Kissinger's second son.

Which brings us to our topic. Paula Kissinger, it becomes clear once more, was the centre of this family, not least for her grandchildren – at least for this one, who visited her every Friday evening and gradually learned the whole story. A small person with an enormous aura. There is only one other person of whom Tom talks with similar respect: his father, he says, achieved extraordinary things.

'And your uncle?' He clearly doesn't like that question. Nothing more about Henry. And it's clear to me that Walter has actually brought his children up and prepared them for life so that they never use their famous uncle's name to open doors for their own careers. When Tom takes me down to the cellar, points out a long wall of shelves full of photograph albums, and shows me one containing pictures of 'Oma' – Grandma – I sense that my relationship with this remarkable family has just been further enriched.

Since I am in the area, I've arranged to see Walter and Genie. The first time I see their house in Huntington on Long Island by daylight, I ask myself: wherever we go, do we take our baggage with us? Once German, always German? Or is it just because I don't know America very well? The area is beautiful and affluent, the properties are vast.

Walter's house is all kinds of things, but it isn't American. It doesn't fit here. It's a European house, at least a hundred years old, built of natural stone, unusually tall for the area, with bays and oriels, covered with ivy. The whole thing looks like a little castle, particularly since it's a little run-down. As soon as we drive in we are greeted by Wolfgang. Wolfgang is the youngest of the Alsatians with German boys' names that Walter has always kept in his home on Long Island.

Walter keeps his motorbike – a heavy BMW, of course – in the garage. And although there's a storm coming, he insists on driving round a few times amidst the thunder and lighting. Walter needs that and because he thinks my crew and I need something

German, he wants to please us and invites us to dinner in a German pub, with a terrible atmosphere and elderly waitresses in dirndls.

If it was up to Genie, Huntington would have been abandoned long ago. They have wonderful residences elsewhere, she says, such as their ranch in Colorado. I can confirm that from my own experience. But Walter doesn't want to give up Huntington. On no account; it's his home. This is the place where his children grew up, and precisely because they have now left home, Walter is fond of this residence. It represents his life with his family, and Walter is a family man. The children and his eight grand-children are the centre of his life, especially now that his working life is behind him. Walter needs the homely, private atmos-phere – very much unlike his brother: 'My desire for a secluded life', he says, 'is not one that I share with Henry.'

For my film, my visit to Walter is very productive. He shows me various local universities on whose boards he sits, and takes me to Topspin, the company in which he is still active as a partner and entrepreneur. This is opportune for me, because these activities are part of his life, and thus part of my film. On the other hand, I don't greatly enjoy the familiar game: when Walter is ready to shoot, we aren't. For example, we can't get our equipment into the car fast enough to keep up with Walter's BMW in the storm. Or Walter would rather talk to me than endure another pan of the camera across his living room with its open fireplace and enormous television, or through the mag-nificent library.

But I do take something with me as I sit once more in the aeroplane on 7 June, a Tuesday, chiefly this: I am getting a better and better understanding of what happened to two brothers who had to leave my country and my city almost seven decades ago. And the closer I get to them, the more I want to know about them; but more important than that, the more I want to know *from* them. Not least from Henry.

On German wheels through an American life: Walter Kissinger at the age of 81 on his BMW bike in Huntington, Long Island, June 2005.

*

So I start a new round. In the summer of 2005 I intensify my contact, I write to Henry, reminding him that he agreed back in April to be filmed with his wife, Nancy. But I soon come to understand that it isn't going to happen. As Genie writes to me, her sister-in-law is 'extremely camera-shy': so much so that there isn't even a photograph of the two brothers with their wives.

At the end of August I call Henry's office and tell Jessee that I'd like to speak to him, just like that. Jessee doesn't see anything wrong with that in principle, but unfortunately she can't help me, not in the morning and not in the afternoon. Henry's gone, or else he isn't back yet. Then all of a sudden she asks me if she and the other people in the office could take a look at my film at some point? 'Sure,' I say, 'of course, when it's finished!' and that gives me an idea: I've promised Walter to come to New York and show him the rough-cut. At the moment we are wondering – Walter, Genie and I – whether we'll finish it before Christmas, before they take their annual trip to California. Why don't I make the same offer to Henry?

However, the film would first have to be presentable. A massive challenge. Normally whole teams of editors deal with this kind of material: four or five people, not to mention the technical apparatus. I am a one-woman crew, with a little studio in my little company, an editor who I work with ten hours a day, and various people I sometimes ask for advice. Otherwise I do everything myself: I research, I write the script and all the commentary, I look for appropriate music, and view the filmed material, which even now comes to about 4000 minutes. On 2 September 2005 I start editing, and with editing come the sleepless nights. Have I taken on too much?

If I have, there's no way back. So I have to keep going. By the end of November I can show the television people in Munich a rough-cut of both parts. And what they have seen, Walter should see. And if Walter sees the film, Henry should have the chance as well, if he wants to. And Henry wants to, at the last minute, when I am already in New York.

On 17 December 2005, a week before Christmas, I've set off again, this time without a camera crew. It's my fifth American trip to do with the Kissingers, and it's the first on which I don't want anything from the brothers – at least, no interviews, photographs or documents. I want to show them something, the first version of the film.

Walter and Genie are anticipating our meeting with excitement and delight. I haven't heard anything from Henry. But nothing ventured . . . So I check in to the Waldorf and after I've had a little rest and a shower I set off. In the hotel I buy a flower as a decoration for a present: on the phone Jessee told me she is going to get married. She is delighted, gives me a hug, and asks if she can get me anything. 'No, thanks.' I don't want to exploit the situation. I later regret that.

Henry isn't there, of course, but Jessee promises to tell him about my visit. Still, he has signed one of his books, which I left there last time with a request for him to do so. So I have a free afternoon, I buy a hot dog and stroll through Manhattan, which is decorated for Christmas. I've heard of it, but never seen it for myself. I am very impressed.

The next morning Anne, Jessee's 'twin' in Walter's office, confirms my appointment with Walter and Genie. Everything is ready and in apple-pie order. They both collect me from the Waldorf. We greet each other very warmly. We are friends. Walter spoke to his brother that morning, and he sends cordial greetings and is very keen to see the film. As soon as possible. But his schedule . . . Henry has also described me once again to Walter as a woman who knows what she wants. He is right there, although I am no longer sure what Henry means by it.

The screening of my film for Walter and Genie takes place in the Princeton Club, and I think to myself, I am gradually getting to know this city through the places that are important for Henry and Walter. At any rate, I prepare Walter for the fact that the film contains everything – the oppression, the expulsion, the fate of the relatives who didn't survive. Walter reassures me; he is 'tough', he says, and he knows the story. I play the film and read out the commentary.

When the first part is over, Genie starts to cry. At first, Walter doesn't stir, then he says – in a quiet, broken voice – that he is deeply moved, and then the tears come to his eyes as well. I am the same. The second part ends with a picture showing the two brothers, around sixty, with their mother, to the sound of the Andante un poco mosso from Beethoven's Piano Concerto No. 5. When the tears flow again – Genie's, Walter's, and mine as well – Walter says he is speechless, and that's not something that happens often. He hadn't expected a film like that. And he will never forget this day. Never. Neither will I. It's what I've been working for; it's made it all worth it.

Later, when we are having dinner at the Waldorf, I ask Walter why he has supported me from the start, why he has tried, in the face of all opposition, to persuade his brother to entrust me with the history of the family. I am pleased with his answer, because it shows me that I was right to rely on a feeling. He liked the way I tackled it, Walter says, the way I approached him, Henry, Genie and the others. And he also says that he has never spoken to anyone about Henry the way he has to me.

Then he adds his impressions of my film, and establishes that he has never seen his brother like that on the screen before. Henry never talks about personal matters on television, because he doesn't like it, and because his position here in America means that he can't. Of course, I mention that I'd also like to watch the film with Henry. 'I think he owes me that somehow.' Walter agrees, but points out that his brother would never set aside ninety minutes to watch something. He wouldn't do that for anyone, not even Nancy. It's in his nature. He can't do it, or

Hold on tight: Henry and Walter Kissinger with their mother Paula, mid-1980s.

he can't do it any more. After a few minutes he would stand up, walk around, or leave the room. He is the same with books. He starts one, sets it aside, and begins the next one.

The next morning Walter calls. He spoke on the phone to Henry, for more than an hour, and told him about yesterday and about my film. And to his great surprise his brother told him he wanted to see me and my film. Above all, he was curious to know what Helmut Schmidt had said about him. Henry didn't have much time, twenty minutes at the most ... Tomorrow morning, at nine o'clock, I was to ring Jessee. Hurray! Later, Walter rings again and tells me how to behave. He is touchingly concerned about me. He knows his brother has just made a big exception.

Needless to say, my appointment with Henry is postponed twice more: from five till half-past, then five again. That's fine by me. I had to rebook anyway. So I start getting ready for my fourth meeting with Henry: short brown skirt, light-coloured top and greenish jacket, pearl earrings. I look great. And that's what Henry says when he greets me in his office. Then the usual: he actually has no time. He is sorry, but tomorrow morning he is going on holiday.

We watch the film on my laptop. To do that we have to sit close together, in a corner of his three-piece suite. I read him the commentary from my manuscript, straight in his ear, so to speak. A ludicrous, unreal situation. I enjoy it. He watches the whole of the part about Fürth like that, complimenting me the whole time. He is amazed by all the things I've found out, particularly about his parents, he says. He is very moved.

Then he looks at his watch, and I am cross. I stop the film. 'You can't do that. You'll ruin the whole mood, and that's what makes the film.' He is surprised, he gives me a sidelong glance and apologizes: it's just that he is always pushed for time. Of course he knows that he has made things very hard for me; but he didn't think I was being honest about it. 'You still don't?' No, he has had too many bad experiences for that, and his brother was rather naive. Did I have any idea what 'they' would have done with this material in America? I can guess. But I am not 'they'.

Now Henry Kissinger knows that too, and he really does have to go. But first he wants to see what other people think of him, and particularly what Helmut Schmidt had to say about him. But then he jumps to his feet, saying that he has given me more than twice as much time as he had planned. Now he has to go. But he promises to watch the film in peace with me on another occasion, and storms out of the door. As I am getting my things together it occurs to me that we didn't say goodbye. I say that to him as I see him taking a look at the stack of messages outside. Henry realizes that's true, so I get another photograph of the two of us together, taken by Jessee.

Later, Walter tells me that Henry has a guilty conscience because of his behaviour, but that he was very impressed and excited by my film, and that he even missed an appointment because of the screening. Then Walter confirms to me what Henry said to Jessee when she was taking the photograph of us: 'We must arrange a date in February or March when I've got more time. I want to watch the whole film with you.' So there will be a next time, and Henry will do something that even his brother thought was impossible: he will watch the whole ninety minutes.

I am happy, and I am also a bit proud. And that feeling carries me through the day, which is entirely chaotic. Public transport has been paralysed by some sort of strike. There are no taxis, and certainly no empty streets. Luckily, I had the hotel book me a car that morning, and when it has finally dropped me off at the airport after a journey at a snail's pace, and I am falling asleep in my seat, I think: I did it – the traffic chaos, and Henry.

*

But my journey isn't quite over yet. The film isn't finished, and discussions with Bayerischer Rundfunk haven't reached a final stage – and, above all, I don't know if I am quite ready to hand it over. The more I think about it during those quiet days, as 2005 leads into 2006, the more honestly I listen to myself, the more clearly I hear a voice saying: the story has assumed its own reality. It hasn't just taken possession of me intellectually and emotionally, it's become interwoven with me, it's become part of my very self.

That feels good, on the one hand. On the other, I am starting to understand that this could represent a serious obstacle on the way to the completion of my film. Could that be the reason why I've been thinking for some time about following the film with a book? At first, it was one of those thoughts that come and go. But at some point it stayed, and on my last trip to America, if not before, the idea became a plan.

I haven't got very much experience, but I know that I can write. I'd never taken on a documentary film of this size, but I was always sure I would be up to the task. Above all, though, I see the function – or rather, the functions – that writing might have for me. I will stay with my story for another year, perhaps two, and if everything goes according to plan, I'll write it from the soul – and be free.

The people whose advice I have been seeking since early in 2006 feel the same. They are a little circle of men who have crossed my path professionally in one way or another at various times. When I show them the rough-cut of my film in mid-January they all say I should insist that ARD broadcast the whole film, all ninety minutes of it. Without being asked, they are all convinced that I should round the whole thing off, and therefore think the idea of a book is a good one.

So I've got my own personal script for the coming weeks and months. First of all, I write to the director general of ARD, insist on a meeting, and get one too. Still, I have been working in public television for decades. Our discussion produces a solution that I can live with: Bayerischer Rundfunk will screen the two-parter, and Das Erste, the major national channel, will show a forty-five minute short version.

For me, that means that I have to think about not just one, but two, even three, versions of my film, because I am also planning an English-language version. That doesn't make things simpler, but it possibly makes them easier: sooner or later the time will come when I can no longer bear to see or hear this story. And then I will finally be able to say goodbye to it once and for all.

First, both versions will have to be completed, and that's why I am doing the final interviews – with Hans-Dietrich Genscher, who immediately agrees; and with Erika Bickert and her husband Konrad, who are completely new to the world of television and who for that reason refused for a long time to appear in front of the camera. But they are among the most important people for my film: Erika and her sister Lore were childhood playmates of Heinz and Walter, and their parents Karl and Babby Hezner were the only ones who stood by Louis and Paula Kissinger after the Nazis came to power. That was why, in his very first letter of April 2003, Walter referred to Erika and Lore, and that's why I am happy that Erika and Konrad Bickert overcome their scruples in February 2006, almost three years later, and speak about this story for the first time.

Around this time I have a run of good luck, because Tom Kissinger stays on the ball, looks for pictures and other documents belonging to his grandparents, and gives me access to them. That's how I get hold of the last photographs of the family before they embarked for America, and later even the recording of a four-hour interview that Paula Kissinger gave to an American journalist shortly before she died, and which is strictly embargoed.

Once again, I am delighted by the family's trust in me, and

inspired by that lovely feeling I enter the final round. All the members of the family who want to, and have the time, are to see the more or less finished film – in New York, of course. But Walter and Genie are still in California, Tom's work is keeping him busy, and Henry, who is so hard to get hold of anyway, has had a fall and given his arm and shoulder a nasty break.

I am all the more surprised then when Jessee calls at the end of March and suggests some dates: Dr Kissinger is willing to watch the whole film. But even Jessee doesn't know what Walter will tell me a few days later: Nancy wants to see the film as well. When he and Genie dined with Henry and Nancy a few days before, to celebrate their thirty-second wedding anniversary, he, Walter, invited Nancy. Of course, he can't guarantee that she'll actually come along. She is very shy, after all.

I am electrified: Nancy Kissinger, Henry's second wife, is a phenomenon. She has hardly appeared in public for years, and, as happens with everyone who shies away from the media for good reasons, all kinds of legends and rumours have grown up around her. For the time being, Walter's message only throws up questions: is there any chance that I might get this woman into my film? Why does she want to see it in the first place? Does she want to appear in it? Or does she want to disparage it to Henry?

Then I am struck, quite unexpectedly, by a feeling that I haven't known for ages, at least not in the context of my film. It's a feeling of grief, or perhaps of melancholy, and it spreads itself despite the joy that I've quite naturally been feeling. What a brilliant conclusion! I'd never have dared to dream that the two brothers would want to watch the film with me, and with their wives.

But it's also the end. If Henry and Walter can see my film and live with it, we have finally found our way to each other.

Then it will mean saying goodbye to a goal that I've had firmly in my sights for over three years and, in the face of all opposition, have never abandoned. The more clearly that enters my consciousness, the more I fear the emptiness that will take hold of me once the film is over and we all go our own ways. So my melancholy mingles with fear of that moment.

Such is my mood that this time, this last time, I don't want to travel alone. I would like to have someone by my side, someone from my group of advisers, to be there for me and catch me if I fall into an emotional state. But no one's available at short notice. One can't, one doesn't want to, a third isn't really in the frame.

So on 10 April 2006 I am sitting on my own in the plane to New York. How many times I've covered this stretch over the past few months. Yet this time everything's different. No joyful expectation, no beating heart. Nothing inspires me, nothing cheers me up. I am melancholy and depressed, in the plane and also in Manhattan. As I go to bed very early, pull the covers over my head, and slip into troubled sleep, I think once again, this time referring to myself: 'Wherever you go, you take your baggage with you.'

Because that is the case, because I've never let things get me down, because I am fundamentally an optimistic person, the world looks different the next day. Once again Walter has a lot to do with it. Admittedly, when he calls late that morning, I've just managed to get myself a sinfully expensive ticket for the Met. But there you go. I'll just have to miss it. Dinner with Walter and Genie in the Princeton Club – where else? – will be far nicer, and more important.

Dinner the evening before the film premiere calms me down and gives me the opportunity to address the plan of the book that will follow the film. Walter has no opinion on the matter at first, but then finds the idea quite plausible and agrees to it. At the same time, I learn a few things about Henry's second wife and their wedding in Acapulco – organized overnight, so to speak – from a first-hand witness. Unlike the journalists, who weren't informed at the time and who were accordingly surprised and annoyed, Walter and Genie were there. So I am prepared for Nancy Kissinger, and also surprised.

For the lady I meet the next day – it's Wednesday, 12 April 2006 – has nothing to do with the picture I've painted for myself of Nancy, the one the public knows her by. When she appears in the public eye she is appropriately styled, an attractive woman at Henry's side. But her appearance in the Princeton Club isn't public, it's private, and I see it as a compliment, an expression of trust: no make-up, her hair hardly done and wrapped in something or other, Nancy – the last to appear, a little bit late – steps through the door. It's immediately clear to me that filming, or even a photograph, would be absolutely out of the question. But Nancy is nice, she greets me warmly and calls me by my name, and then sits down next to us at the table in the legendary Princeton Club.

The other members of the party are Henry, who appears right on time, Walter, Genie and Tom. Then things get going. I translate some parts, and Henry and Walter make spontaneous comments about this and that. Obviously I am particularly excited to know Henry's opinion. He is seeing the full-length version of the film for the first time – and he is great about it, he repeatedly stresses how moved he is by everything, wonders where I found the eye-witnesses, the pictures and the documents, and then says: 'You haven't disappointed me in a single respect. Not one single respect. You have behaved quite correctly. That isn't normally the case.' Later, Walter tells me once again about Henry's reaction: he was very moved. It was a great film, wonderful.

Of course, I grab the opportunity by the scruff of the neck and ask Henry if he would mind me taking the film to other countries. 'No, you can do what you like with it.' And a book of the film? 'Of course, if that's what you want to do.' When Henry asks who the publisher will be, I tell him how things stand, and about the preliminary conversations I've had with my agent.

Then it's all over. After saying a brief farewell, Nancy has disappeared as inconspicuously as she arrived. Tom manages, after three or four attempts, to take a picture of Henry, Walter and me. Henry quickly signs two pictures for me and then has to go. Walter, Genie, Tom and I stay for lunch at the club. The conversation revolves around Nancy. The three of them know each other very well, and I think to myself: no two people are the same. At any rate, Nancy Kissinger wanted to see my film.

In the evening I meet up with Walter and Genie again, this time in the Waldorf. It's a farewell. Certainly, we'll stay in touch and we'll stay close, but it's a farewell. We know we have reached the end of a long journey, one that began three years ago in a London hotel. Later I note: 'A very dignified and beautiful conclusion. A lot of closeness, a lot of warmth. I feel good and profoundly content.'

Before I am driven to the airport the next day I call Jessee again and ask her if I might bring her the lovely bouquet that Walter sent to my room the previous day. Jessee enthusiastically agrees, so I pop across Park Avenue and drop it off. That's a farewell of sorts, too.

What remains is the book. Will it work? Will it work for me? When I start getting my notes in order in May 2006, and approach the brothers to fill some gaps, I receive a rather luke-warm reaction. Not that Henry and Walter have anything against the book; I meet them in New York again to discuss it. But they have done with their return to the past. I understand that. They have been very committed – much more so than I could have expected in my wildest dreams. Now they want to let the story lie.

I can't do that. I haven't yet finished my story, but I know I have to bring it to an end, let it go. The book draws the story from me, page by page. With each sentence I am giving away all that has filled and inspired me, and I wonder: can I fly without this story? Will those wings carry?

Picture sources

Index